abound

A call to purposeful servant LEADERSHIP

Jessie Seneca

I love reading—and writing leadership books. I cannot think of women authors offering leadership books today—bravo, Jessie for venturing into this space. This is a great book on Christian leadership that is not for women only! Jessie does a great job of presenting a Christ-following perspective of biblical leadership. I love her perspective: *The goal of an effective leader involves finding others who have the same passion as you do so that you can build a team that will further your influence and cause together.*

Dr. Hans Finzel
Best-selling author of The Top Ten Mistakes Leaders Make

When asked for examples of good leaders whom I have been privileged to work with, the person who always comes to my mind first is Jessie Seneca. Each event experience with Jessie and her team has increased my respect for her and has helped me grow personally in my understanding of servant leadership. I believe that Jessie was destined to write *Abound: A Call to Purposeful Servant Leadership* for such a time as this. She has managed to distill a lifetime of learning into four chapters with self-development exercises after each chapter to take readers into a deeper understanding and practical application. This book will certainly be one that I highly recommend and will refer to often!

Sue Landis
PHR, CPEC, speaker, Life & Leadership Coach, business executive

Abound presents a biblical challenge for leaders to keep in step with Christ. It's a call that will stimulate you to refresh your vision and stay current with goals. Jessie shares her heart with transparency and provides practical skills to develop your team. Her example calls leaders to be faithful in service and abound in love.

Jewell Utt
Author, speaker, Women's Ministry Director

Jessie's many years of experience as a leader and servant of God comes through clearly in the wisdom and knowledge given through this book. I am thankful for the many different aspects to leadership she presents. This book is effective in both our personal relationships with God as leaders and our relationships with those whom we lead. She reminds us that before we lead, we need to follow the One True Leader. She gives us the tools to start or move forward in the places where we have been called. She also gives us practical ideas in dealing with the challenges of leadership. She has structured this book in such a way that it is useful for an individual or a team to work through.

Erin Rypkema
Women's Ministry Leader

Blessed by almost twenty-five years in ministry, I've read tons of great leadership books and articles, but Jessie's book is unique in its approach and scope. It's readable, achievable, applicable, and inspirational; however, it will also become personal as it highlights the significance of what it really means to be a true servant leader. You'll find yourself reading and re-reading this must-read book as it undoubtedly takes its rightful place in your office as a valuable resource reference.

Donna C. Jacobini
Director of Women's Ministry

Edited by
Fran D. Lowe

Cover Illustration by
Kelly Vanek, Cassidy Communications, Inc.

Interior Design by
Candy Abbott

Published by
Fruitbearer Publishing LLC
P.O. Box 777, Georgetown, DE 19947
302.856.6649 • FAX 302.856.7742
www.fruitbearer.com • info@fruitbearer.com

Unless otherwise noted, Scripture quotations are taken from the New American Standard Bible (NASB) © 1960, 1962, 1963, 1968, 1971, 1972, 1973, 1975, 1977, 1995 by The Lockman Foundation. Used by permission.

Scripture quotations marked KJV are taken from the King James Version of the Bible.

Scripture quotations marked MSG are taken from THE MESSAGE. Copyright © by Eugene Peterson 1993, 1994, 1995, 1996, 2000, 2001, 2002. Used by permission of NavPress Publishing Group.

Scripture quotations marked NET are taken from the New English Translation (NET) Bible copyright © 1196–2006 by Biblical Studies Press, L.L.C., http://netbible.com. All rights reserved.

Scripture quotations marked NIV are taken from the Holy Bible, New International Version, Copyright © 1973, 1978, 1984, 2011 by Biblica, Inc.™ Used by permission. All rights reserved worldwide.

Scripture quotations marked NLT are taken from the Holy Bible. New Living Translation, copyright © 1996, 2004, 2007 by Tyndale House Foundation. Used by permission of Tyndale House Publishers, Inc. Carol Stream, Illinois 60188. All rights reserved.

Scripture quotations marked TPT are from The Passion Translation. Copyright © 2017 by BroadStreet Publishing Group, LLC. Used by permission. All rights reserved. ThePassionTranslation.com.

Printed in the United States of America

To my supportive and encouraging
SHE Leads leadership team:

You make me a better leader
and a more sincere follower
of the greatest leader, Jesus.

Lord, we don't need another book on leadership, I thought when the Holy Spirit put this assignment on my heart. So many good books are already circulating on the shelves regarding leadership (which I read and enjoy). But as a leader, you know better than anyone that when the Lord calls you to do something, you'd better do it. If not, He will find a way to make it happen—with or without your cooperation.

This leadership book is a little different than most on the subject. *Abound: A Call to Purposeful Servant Leadership* has four manageable chapters for the busy leader. My hope and prayer is that not only will you work through this book to better understand your calling and walk, but you will also have the courage to take the leap and build an effective team through the process.

Weekly self-development exercises in each chapter, along with practical insights from noted leaders within their field, will guide you along the way.

abound

These are four suggestions to assist you with choosing your level of participation as you read *Abound: A Call to Purposeful Servant Leadership*.

1. Read the book for yourself.
2. Read the book for yourself and complete the weekly self-development exercises.
3. Read the book with your team.
4. Read the book with your team and complete the weekly self-development exercises.

A more personal note . . .

My earliest recollection of leadership goes back to seventh-grade student government. You know that time in your life . . . when your classmates vote you into student council and you think you have "some" power, but in all reality, the adult adviser calls the shots. It may have been a popularity contest of who was voted in, but nonetheless, I found myself with students from my class, along with the eighth-grade upperclassmen. I wasn't sure what to expect but found myself loving every minute of it—from managing a small budget and organizing an end-of-year dance to putting together a community project committee.

Since those school years long ago, God has taken me through some amazing times of leadership. Most of those times are wonderful experiences, with a couple of not-so-good encounters scattered throughout. Honestly, the tough experiences have indeed birthed this book and the *SHE Leads* conference. Not that I would wish hardship on anyone, but the difficult encounters are those times when I learned the most about leadership. I have read a lot of books and sat under incredible leaders most of my days, but nothing has impacted me more than spending lonely, gut-wrenching nights on the couch digging into the Word of God to refute a decision, or receiving encouragement to march on from the people who came alongside me.

I know we have to go through some of these difficult times, but I would like to share with you through this book all I have learned and hopefully pass on some good qualities and principles as you dream big, walk out your calling, build and manage your teams, or take the next step to fulfill the work God has laid upon your heart.

This is not just a journey but a pursuit to abound in the work of the Lord. Embrace your call. Walk it out with strength. Take the leap and never stop dreaming.

Journeying with Him,

Jessie

"From everyone who has been given much,
much will be required;
and to whom they entrusted much,
of him they will ask all the more."
(Luke 12:48)

Table of Contents

abound

Chapter One

THE CALL

Therefore, my beloved brethren, be steadfast, immovable,
always abounding in the work of the Lord,
knowing that your toil is not in vain in the Lord.
(1 Corinthians 15:58)

But you, be sober in all things, endure hardship,
do the work of an evangelist, fulfill your ministry.
(2 Timothy 4:5)

You've probably heard the phrase, "the call of God," but maybe you don't know exactly what it means. Does the Lord still call people, or was that something He did only in biblical times? The answer is yes, God is still in the business of seeking followers. He places many calls on our lives, and they can be wrapped into two types—lifelong and seasonal. The lifelong call God places on our lives is for each one of us to know Him through salvation and sanctification. Regardless of our skills, talents, or titles, God calls us to be transformed into the likeness of His Son through His gift of eternal life.

God always calls us to a Person and a purpose. The Person we are called to is Christ. Being called to Christ requires the second aspect of that call, fixing our eyes on becoming more like Him every day. This likeness encourages the fruit of the Spirit—love, joy, peace, patience, kindness, goodness, faithfulness, gentleness, and self-control—to be lived out regardless of our life circumstances. As our relationship with Christ grows through the development of habits of reading the Scriptures, praying, and fellowshipping with other Christians, we begin to establish a greater sense of our identity in Him. With that, God begins to reveal or affirm our seasonal callings, which includes a passion and a people.

God has crafted our hearts uniquely to grab onto different passions. Each person is energized by different situations, roles, or experiences. Some feel energized by teaching, others by writing, and some by entrepreneurship. Regardless, God has created you with a passion. Have you caught hold of it yet?

Chances are, if you're reading this book, you feel that God has not only placed a passion and people on your heart, but also an opportunity to lead within that call. This leadership opportunity may have been placed on you, or it may be something you desired. Either way, you are in a position to influence the people who come with your passion.

That's what this book stems from—my personal desire to lead others well and deepen their understanding of what passion and people God has called them to serve, all the while strengthening their ultimate call to a Person (Jesus Christ), and a purpose (becoming more like Him).

When it comes to the passion and people God has or is calling you to, you may feel that you're in a good place. You're currently living in your passion. It's defined and clear regarding the people you're influencing. Maybe you're still unsure of your passion and who it will impact. Or maybe you've found your passion and people, but you're still waiting on God to open up the right opportunity. Regardless, you feel called to lead.

Throughout this chapter, I'll share the story of my personal leadership call to my passion and people. I'll provide lessons I've learned along the way regarding what servant leadership is, how to wait for your call well, and what it can look like to purposefully pursue the passion to lead that God has set in your heart.

For me, I felt called to full-time ministry. However, this call started with my unfortunate personal experience of battling Cushing's syndrome, a rare endocrine condition that is the result of too much of the hormone cortisol in the body. While I was receiving treatment at four different hospitals for four months, a counselor caring for me would pray over me, "*Jessie, someday you will be sharing your experience with others.*" Four years later, while sitting in the audience listening to the speakers at a Women of Faith event in my hometown, the words of that counselor who cared for me in one of the hospitals ran through my mind. It was at that event I felt God calling me into a teaching/speaking ministry. At the time of my illness, it was hard to understand God's will in it all, and even when I felt God's call, I didn't know what it was going to look like. But through years of preparation and many encouraging individuals, today I am enjoying the fruit of my obedience to God through full-time ministry. We'll dissect this more in Chapter Three, "The Leap," so stay with me.

Most of you have probably experienced or viewed from afar how challenging it is to lead effectively. We often hear that a ministry, business, home, or church rises and falls on its leadership. I have even heard it said that people don't leave companies, they leave leaders. *Ouch!*

Good and effective leadership will drive others to stay and want more, not leave. These types of leaders take ownership and live out the mission statements and visions of their organizations every day. I believe that great leadership is ultimately learned. Yes, some are born with an inherent bent toward leading, but even those leaders learn along the way how to develop their skills.

Whether we have titles or not, we're all leaders in some way or another. No matter where you find yourself in this season of leadership in your life, this book is for you.

- The stay-at-home moms or dads managing their families.
- The working person trying to balance it all.
- The leader of a ministry.
- The manager of a business.
- The organizer of an event.
- The president of a company.

I have experienced most of these positions through different stages of my life over the years and have found each one as rewarding as the next. As I look back over the many leadership positions I have held, each one has built upon the next to bring me right where I am supposed to be. Hindsight is a gift because you learn from what has happened in the past, gain understanding for the future, and develop better skills to share with those you lead.

> Hindsight is a gift because you learn what has happened in the past, gain understanding for the future, and develop better skills to share with those you lead.

And through it all, God is bringing you exactly where He wants you—in the grip of His hand, molding you to become a better version of yourself that ultimately reflects Him.

I can remember as far back as the days of seventh-grade student government that kickstarted my love of influencing others, coupled with a desire to make a difference. From organizing an end-of-year dance and fundraising for a class gift, to putting together a community project committee, I loved it all. Now, fast forward decades later. It truly has been an adventure through personal field trips, learning curves, and great successes.

I couldn't always clearly see that undergoing a particular stage of life was for my benefit, so I wanted to move ahead of God at times. Many lessons were learned through the difficulty, despair, and delay that, in the end, drove me closer to the heart of God. I learned not to despise the preparation but rather embrace the wait, accepting delay for what it is—a delay, *not* defeat.

As I shared earlier, my call into full-time ministry required a waiting period. It ended up being a twelve-year journey from the time God placed that desire in my heart until He actually opened the door. During the waiting period, I would sometimes find myself missing God in the here and now because I was preoccupied with anticipating the next season. I needed to adjust my thinking, look straight ahead at Jesus, and let Him write my story instead of me.

As hard as I wanted to control the plan, I was just along for the ride. Oh yes, He gives us our journey, but you and I create the adventurous ride through decisions, choices, and challenges taken.

I'm not going to sugarcoat it—waiting is hard. But as I look back on those divine moments, I realize now that they became the catalyst of His future design, and I am indeed thankful for all He taught me in the waiting room, which prepared me for each next step.

Consider with me some of the benefits that take place in God's waiting room:

1. **Purpose is clarified.**
   While you wait for God to move, don't miss His involvement in your day-to-day activity. He will teach you more about yourself and the purpose He has for you as you seek Him with all your heart. As you work in the calling set before you, each experience will build on the previous one.

   Whatever your hand finds to do, do it with all your might.
   (Ecclesiastes 9:10)

2. **Patience is developed.**
   Sometimes you think that if you can't go right to the big things you so desire, you shouldn't do anything. No, do what is set before you. Be faithful in the small things, and God will build upon them.

   "His master said to him,
   'Well done, good and faithful slave.
   You were faithful with a few things,
   I will put you in charge of many things;
   enter into the joy of your master.'"
   (Matthew 25:21)

3. **Anticipation builds.**

    You tend to appreciate and cherish things the longer you have to wait for them. God gets to display His power in your life to a watching world as His plan unfolds. It will be far greater and beyond all you could ever ask or think.

    > *Now to Him who is able to do far more abundantly*
    > *beyond all that we ask or think,*
    > *according to the power that works within us,*
    > (Ephesians 3:20)

4. **Character is transformed.**

    During the wait, God molds you into the fullness of your destiny. As I look back at this time in my life, if God had opened the door of opportunity when I thought He should have, it would have been a complete train wreck. Maybe, just maybe, you are not ready and God knows it. He is still molding your character into His likeness so when He does open that door, you will be more prepared to display the qualities depicted in Him.

    During the wait, God molds you into the fullness of your destiny.

    > *For this very reason, make every effort to add to your faith goodness;*
    > *and to goodness, knowledge; and to knowledge, self-control;*
    > *and to self-control, perseverance; and to perseverance, godliness;*
    > *and to godliness, mutual affection; and to mutual affection, love.*
    > (2 Peter 1:5-7 NIV)

5. **Intimacy with God increases.**

    In your period of waiting, you will come to know God in a deeper way. Desire to be the best learner you can be. Seek Him with all your heart, and trust Him to complete what He began.

"But seek first His kingdom and His righteousness,
and all these things will be added to you. So do not worry about tomorrow;
for tomorrow will care for itself. Each day has enough trouble of its own."
(Matthew 6:33-34)

I believe that when God closes one door of opportunity, He opens another far greater than what you could have ever expected. They may not have been your initial plans, but they were always God's plans. You just couldn't see them until He revealed them.

Delight yourself in the Lord;
and He will give you the desires of your heart.
Commit your way to the Lord,
trust also in Him, and He will do it.
(Psalm 37:4-5)

Each role or position you may have held has had a different purpose, but each one demanded the same commitment—the commitment of being an *All-In*. One who is an *All-In* is dedicated and purposeful while being a follower of the greatest leader, Jesus Christ.

How you lead is determined by how well you follow. The greatest leaders are the closest followers of the one true Leader. Jesus wants servant leaders to be followers first. Contemporary observers of leadership also acknowledge the need for a leader to be a follower. Douglas K. Smith, acknowledged as one of the world's leading management thinkers and advisers, has written,

In the twenty-first-century organization, all leaders must learn to follow if they are to successfully lead . . . Leaders at all levels and in all situations must pay close attention to situations in which their most effective option is to follow—not because the hierarchy demands they "obey," but because performance requires them to rely on the capacities and insights of the other people.[1]

7

Max DePree, son of D. J. DePree, founder and later CEO of Herman Miller office furniture company, claims that being a good follower is important training to become a good leader. "If one is already a leader," he writes, "the lessons of following are especially appropriate. Leaders understand the essential contributions as well as the limitations of good followers."[2] Leaders must grasp the skills involved with following if they would contribute to those seeking to reach the goal with them.

Following is at the core of being a servant leader. The word "disciple" means "learner." In Jesus' day, disciples literally followed their teacher around as they learned from him. To learn from Jesus means to follow Jesus. The church today, however, seems to be more interested in those who are ambitious to lead than in those who are willing to follow. Leith Anderson, president of the National Association of Evangelicals, makes this observation about the church's obsession with leadership when the overwhelming emphasis in the Scriptures is about following:

> It should surprise us that so much is said about leaders and so little about followers, especially among Christians committed to the Bible. The Bible says comparatively little about leadership and a great deal about follow-ship. Jesus did not invite Peter, Andrew, James, and John to become leaders immediately. He said, "Follow Me."[3]

Jesus called His disciples to follow Him. They became leaders only after Jesus empowered them to lead by insisting they follow Him first.[4] Not only must we follow Christ first, but God also places earthly leaders in our lives for us to follow—some good and others not so much. Regardless, our ability and willingness to follow will make us more effective leaders as we learn, grow, and mature under others' leadership.

So, let's start with whom you are following. Is Jesus your first leader? Or, has He taken a backseat in your daily to-do's of leading? Which earthly leaders has He placed in your life? What does their influence on your life look like? Let's examine these thoughts further as I share some of my personal journey with you.

I recall a time when God opened a door of opportunity to something that I thought would be the most amazing experience. And yes, it started out that way.

But soon after that, it slowly started to spiral out of control to the point that I stepped away one week out from the event, along with a few others.

Leadership styles looked very different from the time I began the quest. It was an eighteen-month commitment that didn't end the way I expected. Or, was it exactly what God ordered?

I vividly remember coming home from the meeting after I resigned and walking into a dark house. My husband had already been tucked into bed for many hours. Honestly, I didn't have the heart to wake him, especially since he had pleaded with me six months prior to step away. These were his exact words: "You will pull out one week before the event."

I thought to myself, *Whaaat? No way. I am doing this for God and not for man. I can do this for the betterment of our community and local women.* So, I marched on . . . .

That heartbreaking night when I resigned, I took my spot on the family room couch and vowed to never do ministry again. *Never*, I said to myself.

The long night soon came to an end with the breaking of dawn. The following days were difficult, but the presence of God and a few friends helped me to continue ahead and hold my head above water.

The event came and went, and if you are wondering, I did attend the event along with 4,800 other women. It was a success, and our community was forever changed by His spoken word. So, what man meant for harm, God meant for good.

I'm sharing this story with you because it is the linchpin to that which I learned the most about leadership: what not to do and who not to be. Yes, through a bad experience, God used all of it—the good, the bad, and the ugly.

This experience drove me to wholeheartedly seek my biggest influencer, Jesus Christ.

It changed the trajectory of whom I followed and how closely I followed. It became more about pleasing God rather than pleasing man. Once I refocused my sight and fixed my eyes back on Him, the author and perfecter of my faith, there was clarity. Yes, Jesus is the example, but He will also surround you with others to encourage you, teach you, and keep pointing you to Him.

The silver lining of this experience was having a dear acquaintance-turned-mentor rise up to come alongside me and spur me on. She was a true portrait of what servant leadership looked like in the midst of chaos. On the day of that challenging event I just shared with you, she was the one who viewed me across the field on my morning walk. After pulling over and parking her PT Cruiser, she walked over to me and cupped my face in her hands to speak truth into my aching heart. She was the one who could see potential in this young woman when I could barely see two feet in front of me. I learned the heart of Jesus and the power of servant leadership. The more time I spent with her, the more I fell in love with Jesus.

Not only was my relationship with Christ transformed, but I learned that whom you follow matters. Do they direct you to Jesus or themselves?

Are they *"I am here"* or *"There you are"* kind of people?

In other words, do they lead their followers selfishly, or selflessly?

Through this experience, I was blessed to sit under this woman's selfless leadership for nearly nine years before she relocated due to a job change. Then, I watched her leadership skills from a distance.

Additionally, others have purposefully and effectively poured into my life through different positions they've held, which was instrumental in developing my leadership style: first, to lead myself well, and then to help lead others to a deeper understanding of their calling. I learned that a call to purposeful leadership starts with you and flows down to those you lead.

Consider the following four ways a leader can pursue purposeful leadership:

1. Walk in a manner worthy of your calling (Ephesians 4:1).
2. Fulfill the ministry set before you (2 Timothy 4:5).
3. Abound in the work of the Lord (1 Corinthians 15:58).
4. Live fruitfully (Mark 4:20).

Walk in a manner worthy of your calling

One day I was listening to a radio show that featured Pastor Chip Ingram from Venture Church in California, who was teaching on Ephesians 4:1, "Therefore I, the prisoner of the Lord, implore you to walk in a manner worthy of your calling with which you have been called." He broke down *calling* like this: we are all called to a Person and a Purpose, but our Passion and People groups are different. As we established at the beginning of this chapter, the Person is Jesus

Christ. This is the main point of the "calling" in this verse: we are all called to the same purpose, which is to emulate Jesus Christ's character. However, we have a different People group that we influence, as well as a different Passion that grabs our hearts. I influence people whom you will never influence, and you influence others who would never know me or listen to me. Yet the goal of an effective leader involves finding others who have the same Passion as you do so that you can build a team that will further your influence and cause together.

Are you purposefully fulfilling your calling to Jesus to love Him with all your heart, soul, and mind—to seek Him first? When you lead yourself well in these categories, others will notice, and you will lead by example. Your daily worship of Him will become a lifestyle worthy of duplicating. Indeed, true servant leadership begins when the leader humbles himself to carry out the mission entrusted to him rather than his own personal agenda.[5]

In the Book of Haggai, the prophet Haggai approaches Zerubbabel, who led the first group of captives from the Babylonian exile back to Jerusalem in 538-539 B.C. After confronting the leadership about the Israelites living in luxury while the house of the Lord lays desolate, Haggai then exhorts Zerubbabel to challenge the people to consider their ways.

While studying this portion of the Scriptures, we also are challenged to consider our ways. Do we just take care of our outward appearance with no regard to what God has entrusted to us, or do we treasure the gift of the Holy Spirit that Jesus Christ left us when He ascended back to His Father? Yes, you and I house this gift in earthen vessels.

Consider your ways. Put Him first and everything else of value will find you, even your calling. When you release your dreams and desires to the One who planted them in your heart, He will be able to work with a vessel for honorable use, set apart as holy, useful to the Master of the house, and ready for every good work (2 Timothy 2:21).

Fulfill the ministry set before you

In 2 Timothy 4:5, Paul encourages his young protégé, "But you, be sober in all things, endure hardship, do the work of an evangelist, fulfill your ministry." We are called to act in a clear-minded way with our decision making and judgments, deal with or accept unpleasant situations, continually share the gospel, and fulfill our call.

Fulfill your calling, not someone else's. God wants you to be purposeful with what He has put in front of you, along with the gift that He has bestowed upon you. At times, we can get caught up in someone else's calling, thinking it's ours to take on. And the truth is, that call is the furthest thing from the heart of God for you. It may be for the other person, but not for you. Once you are able to take your eyes off of another person's calling and focus on what God wants you to accomplish in and through you, you will live a more satisfied and purposeful life.

My husband always says to me, "*Jessie, stay in your lane.*" Staying in your lane keeps your eyes fixed on Jesus and what He wants to accomplish, not what you want to force to happen. It would be remiss of me to say I've never wished for another's calling, or felt slighted because someone was further down the road in a similar calling. But what I learned from that was to be watchful of those who went before me. I watched with purpose and expectancy for what God had in front of me. I tried to take good notes and apply what I learned.

Again, it didn't come without a wait. There is that word again, *wait*. Just as Moses said in Exodus 33:15, "I will not go unless God goes before me," that became my motto. I didn't want to take a step without Him anymore, even if it meant to wait. Then, in Exodus 33:18, Moses continued, "I pray You, show me your glory!" Oh yes, be watchful for His glory with great expectancy. It should all point back to Him, for in Him we live and move and exist (Acts 17:28).

Abound in the work of the Lord

Do you have an Ephesians 3:20 attitude? Do you believe God can do far more above and beyond what you could imagine or think? Indeed, He wants you to live to your fullest potential.

First Corinthians 15:58 tells us, "Therefore, my beloved brethren, be steadfast, immovable, always abounding in the work of the Lord, knowing that your toil is not in vain in the Lord."

First, you need to be steadfast (firmly seated) and immovable (unshaken). When these two qualities are combined within your character, they will propel you, letting nothing shatter your attempt to fulfill your dream, be overcome by your commitment, or take your gaze off the purpose behind the action. You will have the determination it takes as well as the grit needed to do whatever your hand finds to do, so you can do *it* with *all* your might (Ecclesiastes 9:10a).

Second, the phrase, "always abounding in the work of the Lord," is Paul's way of saying, "Continually give yourself wholeheartedly to the work of the Lord." In the Greek, "abound" means "to excel more than; exceed; to overflow." It is a picture of something flowing over the edge on all sides. As you work unto the Lord, you should not do just enough to get by, but rather as much as you can, always abounding in the work He has entrusted to you.

Some people do just what is expected—the minimum. They sit back and watch things happen. Others, out of love, go far above and beyond what is expected. They pour out their lives to overflowing. These people make things happen. They are *All-Ins*! "All-In doing what?" you ask. "The work of the Lord" is the answer. This is purposeful leadership.

And third, be expectant—*knowing that your toil is not in vain in the Lord.* Our Lord's resurrection makes all we do worth doing. And because He sits at the Father's right hand, He has sent His Holy Spirit to abide in you to give you His divine power (2 Peter 1:3). Paul teaches us that the reality of the future shapes and motivates how we live in the present. It gives us purpose to live beyond our abilities and talents, and subsequently, be fruitful.

No matter where you find yourself in your season of leadership, suffer hardship like a soldier, compete as fairly as an athlete, and work as hard as a farmer (2 Timothy 2:1-6), always abounding in the work of the Lord. Galatians 6:9-10 says, "And so, do not lose heart in doing good, for in due time you will reap if you do not grow weary. So then, while you have opportunity, do good to all people, and especially to those who are of the household of the faith."

Live fruitfully

While reading through chapter 4 of the Gospel of Mark, I found myself asking multiple questions: *Do my actions represent my beliefs? What does my life produce? Just how good is the good soil of my heart?* Then, as I reached the end of the parable of the sower, I had more questions on this particular portion of the passage, "And those are the ones on whom seed was sown on the good soil; and they hear the word and accept it and bear fruit, thirty, sixty, and a hundredfold" (v. 20).

What and who determines if you bear thirty, sixty, or a hundredfold fruit? For so long, I seemed to be under the impression that God determined the percentage of the fruit born in my life. Yes, to an extent He does because all things are filtered through His hands as He blesses obedience, but the way you hear and receive His Word will measure the *fold* outcome. It is the responsibility of you, the hearer, to move out of the thirty-fold realm into the hundred-fold. *So, I thought to myself, what does that actually look like? Are you and I living to our fullest potential? Do we produce a hundred-fold?*

In Mark 4, you read about the four soils: hard, rocky, thorny, and good. What is your soil like?

- Hard = no response to the Word sown
- Rocky = emotional response to the Word sown
- Thorny = worldly response to the Word sown
- Good = fruitful response to the Word sown

We measure everything that we hear. When I hear the Word regarding my situation, I determine whether it is received or not, and to what level it is received. I measure everything that I hear. The Word of God responds to my measuring device. Mark 4:24 says, "The way 'you' hear it—the way 'you' measure and respond to it—is the measure that it works in your life." God is not measuring this for you. The man got thirty fold because that is what he heard and responded to. Another man got sixty because that is what he heard and responded to. A thirty-fold mentality never excels to hundred-fold opportunities.[6] But at the same time, we must remember that apart from Him we can do nothing. We must stay connected to the vine because it is the vine that produces the power, not the branches (John 15).

It has taken me many years to understand the purpose in all I have experienced from that first hospital stay. Yet, as I look back over the past twenty-five years with the six surgeries, including a full left pneumonectomy (lung removal) that had to be performed because of the devastating effects of Cushing's syndrome, and the many lessons learned from those experiences, I am determined to practice Philippians 1:21-25:

> For to me, to live is Christ and to die is gain. **But if I am to live on in the flesh, this will mean fruitful labor for me;** and I do not know which to choose. But I am hard-pressed from both directions, having the desire to depart and be with Christ, for that is very much better; yet to remain on in the flesh is more necessary for your sake. Convinced of this, I know that I will remain and continue with you all for your progress and joy in the faith.

Fruitful living will require purposeful steps to accomplish all that God has for you. What do you and I need to do to live in the hundredfold, our fullest potential? Below are six ways we can pursue fruitful living.

1. **Receive, Believe, Achieve** - Hear the Word of God (daily), believe it, and then act on it.

> But one who looks intently at the perfect law,
> the law of liberty, and abides by it,
> not having become a forgetful hearer but an effectual doer,
> this man will be blessed in what he does.
> (James 1:25)

2. **Move beyond the past** - Don't allow past attempts, failures, or fears to stop you from moving forward.

> Once you were dead because of your disobedience
> and your many sins.
> You used to live in sin,
> . . . All of us used to live that way,
> following the passionate desires and inclinations of our sinful nature.
> By our very nature we were subject to God's anger,
> just like everyone else.

But God is so rich in mercy,
and he loved us so much,
that even though we were dead because of our sins,
he gave us life when he raised Christ from the dead.
(Ephesians 2:1-5 NLT)

3. **Goal-setter, Goal-keeper** - Make a list of what you want to accomplish, and then set deadlines. Be specific. Yes, God calls us to make plans and create deadlines, but it's important for you to be flexible when He steps in to nudge your direction.

The plans of the heart belong to man,
but the answer of the tongue is from the Lord.
The heart of man plans his way, but the Lord establishes his steps.
(Proverbs 16:1 [NASB], 9 [ESV])

4. **Know your *Why*** - Know why you are doing what you are doing and be emotionally connected to the action.

Commit your way to the Lord,
trust also in Him, and He will do it.
(Psalm 37:5)

5. **Trust God with the outcome** - Do your part as God leads and then allow Him to complete it. Yes, following Jesus means relinquishing control and allowing Him to take the wheel. He will reveal all that you need to know for each step. Trust Him with the outcome. I found myself writing in my journal today, *Give me the wisdom to search Your plans as I walk in Your ways.*

For we are His workmanship,
created in Christ Jesus for good works,
which God prepared beforehand so that we would walk in them.
(Ephesians 2:10)

For I know the plans I have for you, declares the Lord,
plans for welfare and not for evil, to give you a future and a hope.
(Jeremiah 29:11 ESV)

6. **Make the move** - Pray, pray, pray, and then take the step of faith needed to accomplish all God is calling you to. Hans Finzel, an author of ten books on leadership, says, "Life begins at the end of your comfort zone." (Stay tuned . . . . Chapter Three, "The Leap," is all about this.)

Consecrate yourselves,
for tomorrow the Lord will do wonders among you.
(Joshua 3:5)

. . . it shall come about when the soles of the feet of the priests . . .
rest in the water . . .
(Joshua 3:13)

As you consider this first chapter, "The Call," my prayer for you is that you would establish what God has called you to accomplish, and purposefully pursue His call on your life. Enlist others to help encourage you and walk beside you, and fulfill that call with like-minded people. However, if you are still wondering what your call is, it's okay. Just do what is right in front of you, be committed to the daily reading of God's Word, and develop His character traits.

But beware: there will be others who will try to stop you from pursuing your dreams. Be careful who you share your dreams, desires, and call with so that you will be able to accomplish all God has set in front of you. We should learn to discern what to reveal and what to retain concerning His personal revelation to us. We need to be sensitive to what God wants to keep between us and Him and what He wants us to share. When the time is right, it will be all about the delivery of the message shared in humility so that God will receive the glory.

The Call

Carl Eschenbach
Technology Executive, CA

As I reflect upon my life, I often think about why I always found myself faced with leadership opportunities. It was not until I really started to follow the Lord that I realized it was He who called me to both lead and serve at the same time. During different stages and seasons of my life, God's calling has taken different shapes and forms, but through it all, His fingerprints are apparent. Allow me to share some of it with you.

God's calling on my life to lead started early in my pre-teen years. I found myself having an opportunity to lead through the different athletic teams I was on. Looking back, I found myself playing the role of motivator and encourager of those around me. Also, I was given captainship over almost every team. Although I was unaware of it then, I now realize this was just the start of what the Lord had in store for me. Leadership—His calling on my life.

With years passing, the next tug I felt about this calling was the Lord speaking to me through someone. It was actually delivered through the author of this book and my sister, Jessie. As I watched her grow stronger in her faith and become an amazing mother and wife, it inspired me to get closer to the Lord as well. As Jessie so accurately stated in this chapter, God can work through those serving Him to bring out your calling of leadership. The Lord has a unique way of using His disciples to bring out His calling for His people.

As I began my professional career, like most people I started as an individual contributor. But, upon reflection, similar to my younger years, I found myself feeling that call to lead again. Now, I knew about leadership, but servant leadership—not so much. I wish I did because I would have led differently earlier in my career. However, with time,

I found myself leading in a way that seemed to reflect what I came to know as servant leadership—the idea of leading with the greater good of those around you in mind, having the desire to see others grow, and caring for their needs while pursuing the goal. Once again, I felt this was a clear indicator of God's calling for me to both lead and serve others well. My challenge was that I was just not connected enough to the Lord to know He was steering me in this direction.

Very early into my professional life, I was given an opportunity to step into management. Based on my experience, I was not deserving of this position. It was one of those situations in life when you say to yourself, *"Be careful what you wish for!"* But, as I began to realize this was the Lord's calling, it hit me again. This opportunity was not an accident.

As the Lord called me into the corporate world of executive leadership, I continued to stay focused on expanding my servant leadership skills. These skills were tested, challenged, and even questioned (almost daily). There were days I sat at my desk telling myself, *Stay the course and focus on giving more than getting.*

I would often read John 13:12 (KJV) for encouragement as Jesus

reminds His disciples that He has set an example: to serve. "So after he had washed their feet, and had taken his garments, and was set down again, he said unto them, Know ye what I have done to you?"

What is so powerful about what Jessie wrote in this chapter is that when you serve others, you actually become a disciple to them. You learn as you follow, and then you take your lessons and give them back to your followers. This is exactly what the Lord asks of us. His calling is for us to be His disciples because He knows if we follow Him and His desires, we will, in turn, bring back many to Him in salvation.

Let me give you a personal example of how obedience to His leading brings abundant blessing: I was given the opportunity to be the number-two person at a large technology company for many years. I was part of three CEO transitions. Although I was never given the opportunity to move into the role, each time I remained a disciple of the new CEO, I chose to not complain that I did not get the number-one job.

As a matter of fact, I went the other direction. I prayed every night about being at peace with my personal and professional life. What came out of my prayers was an approach that led me to privately and publicly take on the responsibility to serve the new company leaders and help them become successful. Neither of them had been a CEO before, so focusing on their success was something that drove me. I did this without any regard to what it meant for me personally or professionally. There were times I quietly sat alone and prayed because it felt like I was doing a lot of the heavy lifting and the weight of the world was on my shoulders. It was during those prayers the Lord said to me, *"This is your path. This is My calling for you: to lead others and blessing will return."* By following the Lord's command, I was more than rewarded. The Lord has blessed me more than I could ever have imagined. Thank You, thank You, thank You, my guiding Light.

Some of those blessings were tangible, but the ones that meant the most were not. Actually, two of the most rewarding have been the encouraging words of others and the opportunity to see others experience life-changing events. Hearing a co-worker say, *"There's something different about Carl and his leadership style. He's one of the greatest leaders I have ever seen,"* felt like sweet whispers from the Lord and reminded me that I was merely a reflection pointing to the greatest leader ever to grace the earth—Jesus. I also felt overwhelmingly privileged to play a small role in changing people's lives for the better. How overjoyed my heart would be!

Lord, thank You for calling on me to follow You. You have taught me that to lead others, You must walk behind them. I am right behind You, Lord.

Self-Development

Day One

The Call

We have already established that we are called to a *Person*: Jesus Christ. If you believe John 3:16, you have been called in the truest form and, in turn, Romans 10:13 secures your call to Christ.

For God so loved the world,
that He gave His only begotten Son,
that whoever believes in Him shall not perish,
but have eternal life.
(John 3:16)

For whoever will call on the name of the Lord will be saved.
(Romans 10:13)

Once this most important calling is established, you are called to a *Purpose*: to emulate the character of Jesus.

List the characteristics you are exhorted to emulate and practice from Galatians 5:22-26 and Philippians 4:8-9.

Not only will you want to display these attributes in yourself, but you must also watch for them in those called to join you. Philippians 4:9 has a very demonstrative action verb—*Practice*. In other words, perform these qualities repeatedly and habitually.

Calling, as defined by the Merriam-Webster dictionary, is "a strong inner impulse toward a particular course of action, especially when accompanied by conviction of divine influence; the vocation or profession in which one customarily engages."

Read the following Scriptures and list who was called, who called them, what their calling was, and what their actions were.

Genesis 12:1-8

Nehemiah 2:11-18

1 Samuel 3:1-21

There is a leader, a follower, and a job to complete. The assignment given is not always a desirable one, but one that needs to be completed nonetheless. Like these men called to complete a task given to them by God, He also calls you to be fruitful. How well are you listening?

Have you heard from God the call He wants you to accomplish in this season? If yes, share that call with your group.

If you feel inadequate to fulfill your calling, read Acts 4:13 (NLT):

The members of the council were amazed
when they saw the boldness of Peter and John,
for they could see that they were ordinary men
with no special training in the Scriptures.
They also recognized them as men who had been with Jesus.

Do you feel that God has called an ordinary person to fulfill a God-size job? What have you done recently to fulfill that job?

What does this Scripture say you can have when you spend time with the greatest leader, Jesus? Is this quality evident in your life? If not, what do you need to do to exemplify it?

Has your calling come to fruition yet? If not, how long have you been waiting?

Look up the following Scriptures. Record who waited and how long their wait was. This exercise should bring you comfort during your wait.

Acts 7:17-36

Genesis 40:14 - 41:1; 41:9-14

Luke 2:36-38

Purposeful Action

From today's reading, what area is God asking you to work on or practice?

Self-Development

Day Two
Timeline

Today, I would like for you to trace your life back to that moment you were first called into your particular season of leadership.

On the timeline, write the following milestones:

- **When you felt called into a ministry or vocation. (*If you have not felt a particular calling yet, please still complete the following exercise with the experiences/work you have completed.*)**

- **When your ministry or vocation to others began.**

- **The milestones along the way—good and bad.**

- **The different opportunities you had along the way through your ministry and vocation.**

- **When your attitude all changed from serving yourself to serving others. (Write one word that only you know represents that time.)**

- **Where you find yourself today.**

When you have completed this exercise, under the timeline place the initials of those who have greatly affected your journey—both the good and bad influences.

Now, write the names of those who have poured into or influenced your life, and share with your team their qualities you would like to emulate.

Name   What they helped develop in me

Take a moment and pray for them, thanking God for their influence on your life. Make it your goal to emulate their "pouring," and bless others by exhibiting that same influence.

I am sure you can also think of some people who have not been a good influence in your life. *(I wouldn't dare ask you to write their names, but recall them now in your mind.)*

Yes, we can learn from all of them as well—about what not to be and how not to act. I know for myself that my interactions with difficult people have provided some of the best learning experiences and teachable moments in my life.

Take a moment and thank God for them too, including what you have learned from them.

Purposeful Action
From today's exercise, draw from your life experiences all of those people you are thankful for and write a prayer of gratitude.

Self-Development

Day Three
It's Okay To Be a Follower

Yes, whom you follow does matter. First, you want to be a follower of Jesus and display those characteristics we discussed in Day One. The only way to live these qualities out is to spend time with Him and seek His Word for direction.

Read the following Scriptures. List who the leader was and what the followers' responses to the task were.

Matthew 4:18-22

Luke 9:19-24

Once again, there is a leader, a follower, and a job to complete.
Follow Me . . . . This was a call to service that illustrates the directness,

solidity, and power of Christ's commands. Soon after He called His disciples, Jesus gave them the Sermon on the Mount (Matthew 5–7), an extensive, in-depth teaching on life in the kingdom of God—what you might call basic principles of discipleship, or the Christian life.

Read Matthew 7:24-27. At the conclusion of these verses, what does Jesus emphasize regarding the profound importance of hearing and obeying this teaching?

How have you built your life on the solid rock?

When you build your life on the rock, what will that mean for those who follow you?

Following Jesus also involves following His example. Read John 13:14-17 and share what this Scripture represents.

The lesson Jesus was teaching involves the importance of serving one another in humility of heart and becoming servant leaders. This was a critically important lesson the disciples had been slow to learn, and washing their feet was an extraordinarily effective way of making the point. Sometimes, seeing a concrete example makes a greater impact on people than yet another statement of principle.

How have you seen servant leadership displayed?

What did you learn from it?

How can you tangibly display this kind of attitude to your team?

A servant-leadership approach is one that requires us to lay self aside and care for those we are leading first. It begs of us to lead by example, which means getting our hands dirty, jumping right in, and sharing in the load of those we lead. Our ability to act out of humility demands a certain level of emotional intelligence (EQ). EQ—as opposed to IQ, which is our intelligence quotient—means truly understanding how we come across to others as we lead them. The ability to know ourselves, as well as what others are perceiving about us, is paramount to moving forward with a proposed plan or engaging with the varying personalities that compose a team. It's not a person's IQ that is most essential, but his or her EQ, because it will have the biggest impact on long-term effectiveness in a job—and success as a leader.[7]

If you are just starting out leading others, focus on developing your people skills. Emotional intelligence is the "something" in each of us that is a bit intangible. It affects how we manage behavior, navigate social complexities, and make personal decisions that achieve positive results. Dr. Mick Ukleja, who has pioneered some great work on EQ, breaks down the areas of EQ to understand it better. Ukleja says emotional intelligence is made up of five skill sets.[8]

Review the following skill sets and answer the following questions.

1. **Self-perception** – *Self-perception is the way you view yourself.* As a leader, know your talents and gifts, and with confidence try to use them to their fullest.

   Do you really know your strengths and weaknesses? How do you display them?

2. **Self-expression** – *Self-expression is the expression of your personality as you present a situation.* As a leader, be aware of the way you present your need to accomplish a task. In the twenty-first century, too many are good at just leaving comments, whereas God encourages conversation with Him through prayer and with others as well.

How effective are you when relating to others as a communicator?

Do others understand what you are trying to say to them when you present a task to them?

What characteristics make a person a good communicator?

Would you say that you are a good communicator? Why or why not?

3. **Interpersonal dimension** – *The interpersonal dimension is the art of relaying information within relationships or communication between people.* As a leader, be clear about what you want to relay to your team and how you want them to perceive your request, decision, or challenge.

Do you make it a priority to interact with the people you work with? What does that interaction throughout your day look like?

What people skills are important to you?

4. **Decision-making** – *Decision-making is the action or process of making decisions.* As a leader, there are decisions you will need to make prior to making a presentation to your team. Make sure you think the process through, and invite others to help with important decisions as needed.

What is your thought process as you make decisions for the good of the team?

How can you make decisions in a timelier manner, especially if you linger too long keeping things open?

5. **Stress management** – *Stress management consists of making changes to your life if you are in a constantly stressful situation.* As a leader, it is vital for your well-being to practice self-care through relaxation, prayer, and meditation, as well as exercise.

   How do you act when you are under pressure?

   When you're under pressure, what version of yourself do others see? Is it attractive or off-putting?

   List ways you have learned to practice stress management.

Purposeful Action

   Consider an act of service you can offer your team that, in turn, will show your appreciation.

Self-Development

Day Four

It Starts with You!

A call to purposeful leadership starts with you and flows down to those you lead.

After reading this chapter, where do you find yourself in these four areas listed? Explain how you are intentionally working through each of them.

Walking in a manner worthy of your calling

Therefore I, the prisoner of the Lord,
implore you to walk in a manner worthy of the calling
with which you have been called.
(Ephesians 4:1)

Fulfilling the ministry set before you

But you, be sober in all things, endure hardship,
do the work of an evangelist, fulfill your ministry.
(2 Timothy 4:5)

Abound in the work of the Lord

Therefore, my beloved brethren, be steadfast, immovable,
always abounding in the work of the Lord,
knowing that your toil is not in vain in the Lord.
(1 Corinthians 15:58)

Live fruitfully

Finally then, brethren, we request and exhort you in the Lord Jesus,
that as you received from us instruction
as to how you ought to walk and please God
(just as you actually do walk), that you excel still more.
(1 Thessalonians 4:1)

Depending on your team and work environment, the appropriateness of sharing about your personal life with others may vary. To what extent can your personal faith journey intersect with those of the members on your team?

Read Mark 4:20 again.

"And those are the ones on whom seed was sown on the good soil;
and they hear the word and accept it and bear fruit,
thirty, sixty, and a hundredfold."

What do you need to do to live in the hundredfold (fullest potential)?

Which area (listed below) do you need to work on to help move you into your fullest potential?

1. Receive, believe, achieve
2. Move beyond the past
3. Goal-setter, goal-keeper
4. Know your *why*
5. Trust God with the outcome
6. Make the move

What course of action will you implement to make it a reality in your life?

Purposeful Action

Commit to a specific area that will move you from the thirty-fold mentality to a hundred-fold opportunity.

Self-Development

Day Five

Take Action!

At the end of each chapter, Day Five will be a "take action day" for you and possibly your team, if applicable.

Strategic planning is vital for you and your team. It will enable you to move forward personally and collectively. It is an organization's process of defining your strategy or direction while making decisions on allocating resources to pursue that strategy.

First, determine your personal mission and vision, and then see how it fits into your ministry or organization's mission and vision.

A mission statement describes what a person or company wants to do now.

A vision statement outlines what a person or company wants to be in the future. [9]

The mission is God's call on your life. You know what your mission is when you can complete this statement, *"God called me to:* _____

_____."

Vision is your unique take on that mission. You can state your vision by completing the statement, *"When the mission is complete, it will look like this:*

_____

_____."

How do your personal and organizational mission and vision align? If they don't align, what will you need to do to make the vision clearer?

What are your personal goals?

What are your team goals?

How can you implement the qualities from this chapter to move your vision, mission, and goals forward?

Chapter Two

THE WALK

Therefore I, the prisoner of the Lord,
implore you to walk in a manner worthy of the calling
with which you have been called.
(Ephesians 4:1)

For this reason also, since the day we heard of it,
we have not ceased to pray for you and to ask that you may be filled
with the knowledge of His will in all spiritual wisdom and understanding,
so that you will walk in a manner worthy of the Lord,
to please Him in all respects, bearing fruit in every good work
and increasing in the knowledge of God;
(Colossians 1:9-10)

I recall many years ago, while reading Ephesians 4:1 and Colossians 1:9-10, thinking to myself, *Is it even possible to walk worthy of my calling?* Thankfully, we serve a God who is patient and teaches us along the journey. In the Greek, worthy (*axios*) means "of equal weight."[1] We are supposed to equal the Lord's standards—to be holy as He is holy.

Paul's aim in this petition was practical: a genuine knowledge of Christ reveals a transformed character in Christlikeness. Are you like me, sitting there in your chair wondering, *How can I lead this lifestyle successfully?* Walking worthy of the Lord is a step-by-step process, one that begins by just focusing on the next step. Sometimes we become discouraged in the process because seeking victory seems overwhelming. Yet, if we desire to be the people God wants us to be, our focus only needs to be on the next step—and nothing else. We must walk moment by moment, hour by hour, and then day by day. Yes, we should have the end goal in view, but all He asks of us is to take the next step. We must be obedient to what He is asking for the day in front of us, and then He will take care of what lies ahead.

Of course, there is room for planning, so most leaders will plan their little hearts out. But what I have discovered through my experiences is that a leader who is able to adjust and be flexible with the curves that may come will be able to lead others through obstacles with strength. Strength, not ease. It is never easy to change direction, but if you and the other leaders are able to walk through it with power, strength, and a good attitude, others will follow your lead. A good attitude is the only thing you, as a leader, really have any control over. So, the way you handle a situation, walk out your convictions, and pursue godliness will reveal the level of your daily walk with Jesus.

> Therefore I, the prisoner of the Lord, implore you to walk in a manner worthy of the calling with which you have been called.
> —Ephesians 4:1

If you are trying to walk worthy of the Lord, you may feel that success is elusive. You probably find yourself good for a few days but then trip up. Remember, though, you are in the process of perfecting your walk, and you are no different from anyone else. In fact, we all need the same power that comes from Christ to walk worthy of the Lord. It is His divine power that enables us!

You will recall in Chapter One that I mentioned a radio program with Pastor Chip Ingram's teaching on Ephesians 4:1. Let me expound on that teaching. He simplified *calling* like this: there are four parts to a calling—the first two are the same for each of us, and the second two are different from one another.

44

First, we are all called to a Person and a Purpose. These two are the same for each of us. The Person is Jesus Christ, which is the main point of the calling in this Scripture. In addition, we are all called to the same Purpose, and that is to emulate Jesus Christ's character.

Herein lies our *walk*—emulating Christ's character in how we live. It is what drives our purpose. It is our "true north," for what we believe deep in our core will dictate how we walk, affect our responses, and determine our motives. You and I become whatever and whoever we hold in high esteem.

Second Corinthians 3:18 states, "But we all, with unveiled face, beholding as in a mirror the glory of the Lord, are being transformed into the same image from glory to glory, just as from the Lord, the Spirit." One of the greatest characteristics we can exhibit is a completely exposed openness before God, which will allow our lives to become a mirror for others. Removal of the veil gives us access to God, and then we can constantly reflect Christ's divine glory, which transforms us from glory to glory, making us more and more like Him as we are changed into His glorious image.

There is nothing between us and God. Psalm 34:5 (NLT) says, "When you look to Him for help you will be radiant with joy; no shadow of shame will darken your faces." Yes, it takes a deliberate act of exposure to the Father. You and I need to make it a priority to enter the secret place and walk it out with God. And when we do, He is able to change our approach, attitude, demeanor, and desire.

I believe that one of the hardest battles in a leader's day is the continued practice of carving out quiet time with God. It is very easy to allow the hurried lifestyle of preparing, organizing, delegating, and planning to disrupt one's relationship of abiding in Him. Oftentimes it's something good that will stain it—something good, but not what may be the best. Beware of anything that would spot or tarnish that mirror in you.[2] I know sometimes I can get caught up in the doing and neglect the being. If you find yourself in a similar situation, you may want to consider moving your quiet time to a completely new location—a location away from where you have your daily work, laptop, and to-do-lists. By doing this, you will remove the distractions that vie for your precious attention.

Not only do you want to walk out your calling with great purpose, but you also want those you work with to walk it out as well. As their leader, you must lead by example. You have heard this definition of leadership many times: leadership is influence. Just because someone has a title doesn't mean that person is a leader.[3]

Leadership is a tough road to walk at times because all eyes are on you. It is one for which you will need to draw strength from One higher than yourself. It is not that we need to walk a perfect life, but we should aspire to walk it with excellence and intentionality as our guide.

There is a fine line between perfection and a healthy pursuit of excellence. Perfectionism comes from external comparison, whereas excellence involves satisfaction for achievement that comes from within, no matter what we've done.[4] Perfectionism is focused on "doing the thing 'right,'" if others think it's done right, and how things appear. Excellence is about "doing the right thing." It is focused on the reason for a task, along with the results, for it to be a success.[5]

I love the famous quote by Les Brown, one of the world's most renowned motivational speakers: *"It is better to aim high and miss, than to aim low and hit."* Similarly, Wayne Gretzky, a former professional ice hockey player, was famously quoted, "You miss 100% of the shots you don't take."

God places dreams and desires into your heart. Once He gives you the green light to go after those dreams, you must pursue them with excellence. It is what will distinguish you from someone else who goes after it half-heartedly. Go after your dream with an *"I-will-finish-this-task"* mentality. If you don't take the risk, it may be the one thing you regret at the end of your life.

After writing my first book, *The Secret Is Out*, a Bible study on the Book of Colossians, my husband said to me, *"It's all about finishing. Many people say they are going to do something, but few see it through. It's the last 10 percent that differentiates an average job from a great job. Congratulations on a job well done!"* What he said is so true, but it doesn't come without sacrifice. It may mean you need to free up your calendar, go out for one less Starbucks with a friend, or step away from something for a season to accomplish what is set before you. Set a goal and go after it with the intensity to

> Go after your dream with an *"I-will-finish-this-task"* mentality.

complete it with vigor. Some of your scariest opportunities will be your greatest building blocks to your destiny when you reach beyond yourself and embrace the unknown, which, in turn, will give God the glory as you take on a God-size goal.

Before you can demand excellence from your team, you must aim for it yourself. Every follower wants to know that the person they follow has great determination to move forward with purpose. People don't first follow worthy causes; they follow worthy leaders who promote worthwhile causes.[6]

John Maxwell, author of *The 21 Indispensable Qualities of a Leader*, tells us what every follower wants in their leader: calling, insight, charisma, talent, ability, good communication skills, and character. As a leader, you must understand that you go on display before your followers ever get a chance to see the vision. Once followers gain confidence in you, they will feel confident about the vision.

These are seven assets followers want in a leader:[7]

1. **Calling** – Few things are as compelling as a leader's clear calling. Once you embrace your calling, passion and boldness will follow, and then others will get on board.

2. **Insight** – People respect a leader with insight, which involves wisdom to see issues and vision to see what lies ahead. Although I must admit I don't always clearly see around the bend, I just keep taking the next step in following what God wants from me in a given day. Eventually, He will reveal the bigger picture, but not always at the onset of the vision.

3. **Charisma** – People flock to leaders who make them feel good about themselves. Continue to help others see the significance of their roles on your team, as well as the giftedness they bring with them. This is another true sign of someone with strong emotional intelligence.

4. **Talent** – Look no further than the entertainment industry for evidence that followers swarm around talent. Continue to develop the talents and gifts God has given you to the best of your ability,

and then encourage your team members to do the same. (You will take a spiritual gift test in Chapter Four.)

5. **Ability** – People feel a natural attraction to those who can get things done. Display and practice your abilities, and others will follow.

6. **Communication skills** – A leader who cannot communicate his calling and vision has trouble getting anyone to buy in to his leadership. However, when you effectively share your vision, others will catch it and be able to communicate it as well.

7. **Character** – It takes character to win and maintain trust. Followers want to see that you can stand strong and display courage in the face of adversity. Make sure your anchor is secure in Jesus so that when the strong winds come, you will be able to remain steadfast. Not only is character important in the difficulties, but more so in the successes. Proverbs 27:21 (NLT) says, "Fire tests the purity of silver and gold, but a person is tested by being praised." A man's response to praise is a test of his character.

When leaders take charge, the people gladly follow. Praise the Lord! (Judges 5:2 NLT).

These seven assets must be continually set before you and put into practice. No matter if they are eighteen or eighty-five years of age, good leaders continue to sharpen their skills and learn from those who have gone before them. Psalm 86:11 says, "Teach me Your way, O Lord; I will walk in Your truth; unite my heart to fear Your name." This Scripture pulls out three key lessons and expounds on the list from Chapter One's pursuit of purposeful leadership, which will inspire our determination to walk out our individual callings with great purpose.

Three lessons learned from Psalm 86:11:

1. **"Teach me Your way"** – It all starts with allowing God access to our

hearts, minds, bodies, and souls. You and I must yearn to live for Christ, cherish His Word, and strive to put it into practice. Once you commit to knowing the Father's heart through the (daily) study of His Word, you will be able to apply it to yourself and your team. Whether or not your work is in ministry or a secular environment, reading His Word will dramatically impact your leadership more than any other book or resource. Ask God to open your mind to understand the Scriptures (Luke 24:45). The greatest leaders are the closest followers of the One True Leader.

Purposefully live out what you learn as an example to your team.

2. **"Walk in Your truth"** – Again, herein lies our *walk* . . . . So we must emulate Christ's character in how we live. First John 1:7 tells us "to walk in the Light, as He Himself is in the Light." To walk in the Light means living in obedience to God's commandments. Two benefits result from walking in the Light: fellowship with other believers and the continual cleansing from sin. When we walk with God, we enter the dimension where God unfolds the secrets of His kingdom and a daily direction to follow. Not only do we want to walk out our individual callings with greater purpose and integrity, but we also want those we work with to walk it out as well.

Purposefully meet with God each day for direction. Missing this step will hinder your leadership and may even take your eyes off of what is important.

3. **"Unite my heart to fear Your name"** – Desire to have an undivided heart that is completely devoted to the Lord above all else. Love Him as your first and forever love. Strive to allow your heart's desires to fall in line with the Lord's, continually testing your motives against His will. Bear each other's burdens and share each other's joys. Romans 15:5-6 (NIV) says, "May the God who gives endurance and encouragement give

49

you the same attitude of mind toward each other that Christ Jesus had, so that with one heart and mouth you may glorify the God and Father of our Lord Jesus Christ."

Purposefully commit to unite your heart with God's will, and pour out that same love to your team members.

When you purpose in your heart to learn from His ways, walk in His truth, and unite your heart to His, He will make a way when there seems to be no way. This is a choice you will continuously need to make, and no one can make it for you. But, I promise if you take to heart these three lessons, your work will have higher impact and greater influence.

As you walk out these principles, your team will observe your commitment, and you will gain their trust. Stephen R. Covey, author of *The 7 Habits of Highly Effective People*, says,

> Trust is the foundation of all effective relationships and organizations. Without a culture of high trust, true empowerment can neither be established nor sustained. Why, then, is the trust level in most organizations so chronically low? The reason is that trust is not the result of organizational imperative or program. In other words, it is not a quick fix. It is the fruit of trustworthiness at the personal level.[8]

Max DePree explains that building trust in organizations "has become a chief responsibility of leaders, an essential duty especially in the eyes of followers."[9] Warren Bennis, a pioneer in the contemporary field of leadership studies, claims that trust is one of six basic ingredients of leadership, as it also is a product. It is the one quality that cannot be acquired, but must be earned. It is given by coworkers and followers, and without it, the leader cannot function.[10] Trust is the foundation upon which relationships in every setting is built. Trust between leaders and their followers allows the work to be done and the mission to be achieved. Trust destroys an atmosphere of control and creates an air of freedom. Trust allows the leader to lead.[11]

As you walk out these principles, others will observe the work of Christ in your life and want to emulate your character. It will become a ripple effect to those on your team. Then, as you and—if applicable to your work—your team strive to walk in a manner worthy of Christ, your impact will increase on those you serve in the church, workplace, or ministry.

Now that we've unpacked the Person and Purpose from Ephesians 4:1, let's explore the remaining two aspects—a Passion and a People. These aspects will be unique to each one of us; however, it's essential that while building and leading our teams, we enlist others who share in the same Passion but different People. Having team members with a similar Passion will take our cause deep, but having team members with different People will widen the scope of our influence.

Be assured, it will take a watchful eye to develop a good team. Once your team is established, you will move forward with accelerated momentum. "Oh," you ask, "what if I am joining an established team?" If you're joining an established team, consider doing your homework on that team. Are they a united unit? Do they have the same goals? Are they welcoming and accepting of new team members? You can never be 100 percent sure you are a good fit until you spend some concentrated time with them, but if God is leading you in that direction, it is worth the chance.

Part of our role as leaders is to keep the passion ignited within our teams. This is just one of many reasons why it's important for us to stay connected with our followers. It's our job as leaders to have a sense of whether or not our followers still feel called to the Passion they had when we enlisted them. If over time their fervency fades or seems to change, we will need to share our observations with them.

This change in passion isn't always a bad thing. I'm sure you can look back over your life and see how your passions have taken twist and turns. However, if the passion is lost and the individual is harming your mission, it is your responsibility to ensure the health of your team. This may require a challenging conversation and strong action; however, it will be necessary for preserving your team's goals.

It is also the responsibility of us leaders to check our own motives and passions. Like our followers, our individual passions can also change as God calls us to different seasons of leadership. We owe it to our team, organization, or business to be honest with ourselves about where we are.

In the end, leaders do more damage by staying too long than by leaving too soon.[12] Dr. Hans Finzel, a trusted authority in the field of leadership, gives the seven motives for why someone will hang onto a position even when their passion is gone. He states multiple reasons a person's passion may fade.[13]

1. Power

2. Prestige

3. Position

4. Popularity

5. Pride

6. Personal gain

7. Paycheck

Some team members may not own up to their lack of passion, but if you see a member going down this road, you will want to bring it into the light. It is not always a bad scenario. Just as people are called into a position, vocation, or ministry, they can also be called out of that same position, vocation, or ministry.

When you're passionate about something, no one has to make you do it. You're willing to get up early, stay up late, and do it for free. Passion isn't dependent on position, title, things, or people—it comes from within. It's about that twinkle in your eye and the spring in your step. Passion involves a new vitality, meaning, energy, purpose, outlook, and hope! After all, "The same spirit that raised Jesus Christ from the dead lives in us" (Romans 8:11). You can't find that kind of passion on a shelf or take it in pill form. Passionate living is part of the external evidence of the internal presence of Christ in you.

Colossians 3:23 reminds us, "And whatever you do, do it heartily, as to the Lord and not to men." This passion is so big, it encompasses all of our lives—both sacred *and* secular. This includes things we must do (like working and cleaning the house), things we choose to do (like fun and family), things we're commanded to do (like loving God and loving people), and anything else we're called to do.[14]

One thing I have learned is that you never want to talk someone into taking a position or keeping a position. It is better to have a particular role unoccupied than fill it with the wrong person. Personally, I have been called out of positions I thought I would maintain for life. It was never easy. But for me, once I made the decision to step away, there was a peace that passed all understanding because I knew I had made the right decision.

While working through Priscilla Shirer's Gideon Bible study, I came across this very pertinent question, which came at a pivotal time in my life: *"Are you holding onto something God is asking you to release?"* Wow, this question rocked my early morning time with God. You know, that time in the middle of the night when you can't sleep . . . 2 a.m. time . . . and you feel God nudging you to spend time with Him. I wiggled my way out of bed, hit my couch, and began to listen to His still, small voice.

I must admit, it is not what you always want to hear, even though you know you are hearing Him loud and clear. What do you do with what you hear? Obedience is what God wants. Obedience shows that you recognize God is in control and you will trust Him with the outcome. Removing myself from a loved position was not what I wanted, but it is what God desired. And over time, I saw the bigger picture.

There is a difference between hearing God and truly listening to Him. I wonder at times, *How well do I listen to God, or do I just merely hear Him as* blah, blah, blah? Some days, you can go through your morning devotions in rote fashion without really listening to what God wants you to hear from Him. Do you desire to be more like Samuel? First Samuel 3:9-10 tells this story: "And Eli said to Samuel, 'Go lie down, and it shall be if He calls you, that you shall say, "Speak, Lord, for Your servant is listening." So Samuel went and lay down in his place. Then the Lord came and stood and called as at other times, 'Samuel! Samuel!' And Samuel said, 'Speak, for Your servant is listening.'" We must cultivate this attitude within our hearts: "Speak, for Your servant is listening."

First, for someone to speak with you, you must be in a relationship. Second, you must have a servant-hearted attitude and know your place before God. Third, you must have an open ear to hear what God is saying to you, and really listen to Him. Finally, you must act on what you hear from God. The way we hear God today is through the reading of His Word. The more you read His Word, the more you will understand His will for your life, and then your walk will start to align with His ways.

The distinction between listening and hearing is this: Hearing is always occurring, most of the time subconsciously, *and in the case of hearing the indwelling fragment of God, it always occurs in the superconsciousness.* In contrast, listening is the interpretative action taken by the listener. Hearing is simply the act of perceiving sound by the ear. If you are not hearing impaired, hearing simply happens. Listening, however, is something you consciously choose to do. Listening requires concentration and action.[15] This is why it is important to meet with God in the quiet place of His presence and listen for His still, small voice. If you listen to what He tells you in the darkness, then speak it in the light; and what you hear *whispered* in *your* ear, proclaim upon the housetops (Matthew 10:27).

I am sure you desire to be a faithful leader and good listener as you follow God, or you would not be reading this book, although at times I know it is easy to get caught up in the doing and neglect the *being.* It is in the *being* where you will hear His still, small voice and then have to make a decision to listen and act upon it. Don't become so preoccupied with accomplishing the task at hand that you miss the experience along the way. It is in the experience where you meet God. It is through the small decisions that great things are fulfilled. Never despise the day of small beginnings and forget where you have come from or what God has brought you through.

The Shorter Westminster Catechism asks this question, "What is the chief end of man?" and answers it this way: "The chief end of man is to glorify God and enjoy Him forever." Our primary task in this world is not to only be workers, but worshippers. A. W. Tozer, who suggests that worship was the missing jewel of the evangelical church, put it like this: "We're here to be worshippers first and workers second. We take a convert and immediately make a worker out of him. God never meant it to be so. God meant that a convert should learn to be a worshipper and after that learn to be a worker. The work done by a worshipper will have eternity stamped on it."

We clearly see this depicted in the famous story of Mary and Martha. Martha, bustling about in her kitchen, is frustrated and distracted because her sister Mary is listening at the feet of Jesus rather than helping her get things done. Jesus, with characteristic insight, draws a line between the urgent and the important when He says, "There is only one thing worth being concerned about. Mary has discovered it—and I won't take it away from her!" (Luke 10:42 TLB). Martha's concern about being hospitable is not ignored by Jesus; He simply highlights that when it comes to priorities, worship comes first and work second. So, let's draw a line and reach a definite conclusion before moving any further—our worship of God should take priority over our work for Him.[16]

Once, while speaking at a leadership conference, someone asked this question of our panel, "I have been observing your team all day and wonder how you can be so gracious in your actions?" We looked at one another with a question in our eyes, *Who is going to answer this one?* Silence fell over us for what seemed like eternity, but it was actually only about ten seconds. I grabbed the microphone with confident hesitation and answered, "You never forget where you have come from, and always make Jesus your priority over your position."

One Scripture I always have at the forefront of my mind when addressing a group, speaking at a conference, organizing a team, or leading a meeting is Proverbs 3:3: "Do not let kindness and truth leave you; bind them around your neck, write them on the tablet of your heart."

Yes, wear kindness as a necklace. If you do this as you enter a room, you will look at those in front of you differently and be gracious to them. You will see them through Jesus' eyes. In turn, your walk will be obviously different than that of others. Remember, your goal is "to *walk* in a manner worthy of the Lord, to please *Him* in all respects, bearing fruit in every good work, and increasing in the knowledge of God" (Colossians 1:10).

A Pure Heart

Sue Landis
Speaker, Life & Leadership Coach,
Business Executive, Pennsylvania

As Jessie shared, we are called to a Person and a Purpose. It was during a three-day personal retreat in August 2014, after more than thirty-five years in women's ministry, that God revealed I was "out of sync." How did I get there while trying so hard to walk in a manner worthy of my calling? It was during this time that God revealed the solution to me— *"becoming in sync with my life purpose"* was vital for me to move forward.

Now, please don't be too shocked when I admit there are times, even though I say I believe God's Word is truth, when I don't really live like I believe it. This "becoming journey," as I refer to it, is a lifelong journey—not a destination!

During my personal struggle with rejection and longing to be understood in my leadership role, Jarod, a business consultant and coach, suggested that I may have a divided heart instead of a pure heart. *Ouch!* My flesh wanted to reject this insight, but the Holy Spirit confirmed that understanding this was the next step in my journey of *becoming in sync.* Jesus always responded with a pure heart—He never sinned!

Pastor Armond Weller gave me, as a new believer, the illustration of putting God on the throne of my life and allowing the fruit of the Holy Spirit to freely flow through me. He encouraged me not to allow my spiritual hose to get "kinked." The picture of how a garden hose gets kinked, thus preventing the water from flowing through to nourish the plants, has served as a guiding principle for me. If my heart is divided and not pure, my spiritual hose will be "kinked," and His qualities won't be evident to others.

As a Christian serving in various leadership roles ranging from the marketplace to church, I experience many distractions as I seek to know my calling, walk out that calling, and even as I take the leap to obey God's call! Jessie has done a beautiful job of sharing so many aspects of servant leadership by giving us self-development exercises to help us strengthen our foundation by applying what God reveals to us through the reading of her chapters. It was through the completion of the self-development exercises that I was reminded how important it is for us as servant leaders to keep our hearts pure and our spiritual hoses unkinked.

According to Søren Kierkegaard's book, *Purity of Heart Is To Will One Thing*, a divided heart will cause us to get tangled up with the distractions and kink our spiritual hoses. There will be well-intentioned people who love us and the Lord but will not understand a fully committed heart. At times, we may be misunderstood and rejected. However, we are called to humility with an undivided heart, to will one thing—giving a correct representation of Jesus.

So, God calls us to allow the fruit of the Spirit to freely flow through us to those in our sphere of influence— *the fruit of love, joy, peace, forbearance, kindness, goodness, faithfulness, gentleness, and self-control* (Galatians 5:22-23a NIV). Likewise, as Jesus was able to love the unlovable, forgive the unforgivable, and encourage even those who did not want to receive encouragement, I seek to walk out these same characteristics in my life and *become in sync with my life purpose of glorifying Him.* Praise God, 2 Peter 1:3 tells us that He has given us everything we need for life and godliness to live with a pure heart!

The Walk

Verna Bowman
Speaker, Author and Avid Journaler
www.vernabowman.com

Is it possible to walk worthy of our calling—no matter what?

I remember the moment I was called to women's ministry leadership. Uncertainty seemed to outweigh the excitement. I questioned how a broken life could possibly be useful to anyone and couldn't see how I could be an effective leader in the midst of facing many challenges within my family. However, there was an unshakable sense to go forward, where I soon discovered that when we live out our weaknesses before others, it demonstrates strong leadership. God will use it not only in our lives but in those who are watching. Walking in faith during painful seasons is instrumental in leading others to trust Him more.

It's inevitable that all of us will experience some form of loss or hardship—but can we faithfully lead when we feel like life is falling apart? As leaders we may feel that we're responsible to hold it together in order to help others walk through the hard places. Yet it is only through radical dependence on the One who does hold it together that we will know how to persevere or when to pause for a time. Strong leaders understand the need of surrounding themselves with trustworthy mentors.

I'm grateful to have had a good mentor—Jessie Seneca. In the late nineties, Jessie met with me as well as two other women who were passionate about developing a ministry in our church. One of the most effective ways that she equipped us to lead well was by her steadfast example.

The goal in ministry is to work together in unity and encourage those we serve to do the same. When we face times of opposition, conflict, or criticism, it's important to stay near to those who will cheer us on to faithfully respond in grace. We need to support one another when we grow weary and passion begins to fade. In other words, we need to walk together.

However, our priority must involve time alone in His Word as followers rather than leaders. Our devotional lives sometimes get pushed behind the teaching, planning, speaking, and doing. If we're not intentional, it will rob the sacred space that belongs to Him when we simply listen to what He has to say to us. Walking out our calling with purpose and remaining on track begins with a close walk with our Father. When we fix our gaze on Him, we will not only walk but run toward the goal of a true leader—to help others follow Jesus. I will keep my eyes on Jesus, my leader (Hebrews 12:2).

Self-Development

Day One
Your Walk

Read the following Scriptures and describe what your walk should resemble.

Genesis 5:22-24 (NLT)

Proverbs 13:20

Micah 6:8

John 8:12

Galatians 5:16, 25

Ephesians 5:1-2, 8, 15

While the writers of the Scriptures use many vivid metaphors to describe the Christian life, by far the most common one is a walk.

How does the metaphor of walking with God appeal to you? How will your walk affect how you lead?

What next step does God want you to focus on today? Personally? Corporately?

There are some days you won't feel like taking the next step out of fear, inadequacy, or obstacles in your way. Martin Luther King Jr. said, "We must keep moving. If you can't fly, run; if you can't run, walk; if you can't walk, crawl, but by all means keep moving." At times you will need to ask others to help you move from here to there. Together you will accomplish more than you can do on your own.

What would it take to be excellent (not perfect) at what God wants to accomplish through you and your team?

Read Philippians 3:14 and 4:13 and write your formula for accomplishing a God-size dream.

Courage, grit, resilience, focus, perseverance, and conscientiousness may be some of the aspects in your formula, but without pressing through in Christ's strength and power, you will not be able to accomplish all He has for you.

Purposeful Action
What next step will you take to accomplish your God-size dream?

Self-Development

Day Two

His Word Is Truth

Today's personal development exercise is purely Scripture look-up. Proverbs 25 through 31 is directed toward leaders. *For additional reading, read a proverb a day from chapters 25 through 31 for the next seven days and record all your findings in the column or in a separate notebook.*

Write next to each Proverbs message how you can personally apply it. Also, you can use these principles to observe those with whom you are building your team.

Proverbs 25—31

Proverbs 25:6-7 (TPT)
Don't boast in the presence of a king or promote yourself by taking a seat at the head table and pretend that you're someone important. For it is better for the king to say to you, "Come, you should sit at the head table," than for him to say in front of everyone, "Please get up and move—you're sitting in the place of the prince."

What is the message?

What is the application to you?

Proverbs 25:27 (NET)
It is not good to eat too much honey, nor is it honorable for people to seek their own glory.

What is the message?

What is the application to you?

Proverb 27:2 (MSG)
Don't call attention to yourself; let others do that for you.

What is the message?

What is the application to you?

Proverbs 27:21 (NLT)

Fire tests the purity of silver and gold, but a person is tested by being praised.

What is the message?

What is the application to you?

Proverbs 27:17 (NIV)

As iron sharpens iron, so one person sharpens another.

What is the message?

What is the application to you?

Proverbs 27:23 (NIV)

Be sure you know the condition of your flocks, give careful attention to your herds . . .

What is the message?

What is the application to you?

Proverbs 28:2 (NIV)
When a country is rebellious, it has many rulers, but a ruler with discernment and knowledge maintains order.

    What is the message?

    What is the application to you?

Proverbs 28:26b (NIV)
He who trusts in himself is a fool, but he who walks in wisdom is kept safe.

    What is the message?

    What is the application to you?

Proverbs 29:1 (NLT)
Whoever stubbornly refuses to accept criticism will suddenly be destroyed beyond recovery.

    What is the message?

What is the application to you?

Proverbs 29:18 (MSG)

If people can't see what God is doing, they stumble all over themselves; but when they attend to what he reveals, they are most blessed.

What is the message?

What is the application to you?

Purposeful Action

Discuss your data with your team and encourage one another.

Self-Development

Day Three

With Purpose

What were your thoughts when you read this quote from Les Brown, *"It is better to aim high and miss than to aim low and hit"*?

If God is asking you to go after your dream with an *"I-will-finish-this-task"* mentality, how are you performing the task?

Have you fallen short of aiming high? If yes, what will it take for you to refocus?

Rank from greatest to least what you feel your strengths are regarding the seven assets followers want in a leader: calling, insight, charisma, talent, ability, communication skills, and character. (Take a peek back on pages 47-48 for the descriptions of each.)

       1.

       2.

       3.

       4.

       5.

       6.

       7.

If you are working through this book as a team, write next to each asset the person from your team who best represents this quality.

Assets	Name
Calling	
Insight	
Charisma	
Talent	
Ability	
Communication skills	
Character	

Take time to encourage your team members with your assessment.

Which of the three lessons to purposeful leadership from Psalm 86:11 ("Teach me Your way, O Lord; I will walk in Your truth; unite my heart to fear Your name") do you need to tackle this week? How will you purposefully accomplish it?

Teach me Your way

*I purposefully plan to*_____.

Walk in Your truth

*I purposefully plan to*_____.

Unite my heart to fear His name

*I purposefully plan to*_____.

In the Book of Ruth, the title character walked out her commitment to her God, mother-in-law, and Redeemer with purpose and resolve. Her reward, beyond her redemption, was her reputation. She was known by all as a *woman of excellence* (Ruth 3:11).

Read Ruth 2:10-12 and list the virtue for each verse.

v. 10 _____

v. 11 _____

v. 12 _____

Ruth had great respect for Boaz. Boaz noticed her character since her reputation preceded her. Therefore, Ruth was rewarded with a great blessing spoken over her.

As with Ruth, how is God asking you to walk out your calling with great purpose and excellence?

Purposeful Action
Take the next step closer to accomplishing what God has asked you to do with an *I-will-finish-this-task* mentality.

Self-Development

Day Four

Focus

I am sure as you look in the rearview mirror, hindsight is 20/20. As I've already stated, hindsight is a gift because you learn from what has happened in the past, gain understanding for the future, and develop better skills to share with those you lead. At times, though, you can become stuck in the past, looking either at failures or successes. Yes, draw wisdom from all the experiences to move forward with better insight; however, you may need to refocus on where God is taking you in the future. Søren Kierkegaard, a Danish philosopher, theologian, poet, social critic, and religious author, said it best when he wrote, "Life can be understood backwards, but it must be lived forward."

Read Philippians 3:12-14. What does Paul say he must do?

Yes, it is good to celebrate accomplishments and relish in the goodness of God for a job well done, but just as you don't want to get stuck in the mire of past failures, you also can't stay wrapped up in the present successes either. God is always doing a new thing, so He may be asking you to reinvent yourself, your ministry, or your organization.

What will it take to get you out of the rut of focusing on past failures or present successes?

Look up the following Scriptures and describe the action needed to be taken.

Matthew 14:23-33

John 6:15-21

1 Corinthians 9:23-27

Isaiah 43:18-19

All of these Scriptures have one thing in common: make a move. God is asking us to be willing to step out, receive Him in, run with purpose, and be watchful for new beginnings. In order to step out with clarity, though, first you must focus on His vision.

Read the following Scriptures and write what and where your focus needs to be.

Proverbs 4:25-27

2 Corinthians 4:18

Hebrews 12:2

Please read Proverbs 4:25-27 from The Passion Translation (TPT):

> *Set your gaze on the path before you.*
> *With fixed purpose, looking straight ahead,*
> *ignore life's distractions.*
> *Watch where you're going!*
> *Stick to the path of truth,*
> *and the road will be safe and smooth before you.*
> *Don't allow yourself to be sidetracked for even a moment*
> *or take the detour that leads to darkness.*

What are some distractions that are keeping you from fixing your eyes on the path in front of you?

How are the distractions beneficial?

How are the distractions reasonable?

If the distractions are either beneficial or reasonable, be discerning about the voice of God, as He says, "Your ears will hear a word behind you, 'This is the way, walk in it,' whenever you turn to the right or to the left" (Isaiah 30:21).

Even though some may want to stop the work the Lord has set in front of you, stay strong to the call placed before you, and be as perceptive as Nehemiah: "For all of them were trying to frighten us, thinking, 'They will become discouraged with the work and it will not be done.' But now, O God, strengthen my hands" (Nehemiah 6:9). Joshua also encouraged the Hebrews, saying, "Be strong and courageous! Do not tremble or be dismayed, for the Lord your God is with you wherever you go" (Joshua 1:9).

Purposeful Action

Is God asking you and/or your team to step out with Him for a new thing? What will you do to take the first step?

Self-Development

Day Five
Take Action!

At the end of each chapter, Day Five will be a "take action day" for you and your team. Evaluate your walk and make the necessary changes if needed from the previous four days.

What steps will you and your team take to have an "*I-will-finish-this-task*" mentality?

1-year goal

6-month goal

3-month goal

1-month goal

Thank God for the invitation to walk with Him. Trust Him to lead, and focus simply on your next step. Ask Him to show you what to accomplish today. Ask Him to help you quiet the other voices vying for your attention, and then listen for His voice.

Chapter Three

THE LEAP

Commit to the Lord whatever you do,
and he will establish your plans.
(Proverbs 16:3 NIV)

R eady or not, *let's go!*

- Have you picked up this book with a dream in view?
- Has God put a desire deep in your soul, yet you are still waiting for the open door?
- Do you find yourself questioning God's timing?

No matter where you find yourself, know this: God is in control. Nevertheless, taking the leap to pursue the call God has laid on your heart can be scary, lonely, and exhilarating all at the same time.

If you are like me, you can look back and see the beginning of God's plan. You may not have realized it was His plan at the time and possibly even wondered why it was happening. But over time, you embraced it as a divine process to bring you into this very season of your life and the fullness of your destiny. Do not despise the small beginnings because that's where it all starts. The place of small beginnings is where God births ideas for grander things to come.

Before stepping onto the moon's surface for the first time, Neil Armstrong uttered a famous quote that has great depth: "That's one small step for a man, one giant leap for mankind." In the same way, you only need to focus on the first step in order to open up greater opportunity ahead, and then allow the steps that follow to turn into the leap. Be faithful with what is right in front of you, and the next step will be revealed in His time.

Your one act of obedience may not only impact those who walk with you but a generation that follows. In 1996, while I was sitting in the audience listening to the speakers at a Women of Faith event in my hometown, the words of a counselor who cared for me in a hospital for three months during my illness ran through my mind: *Someday you will be sharing your experience with others.* It was at that event I felt God calling me into a teaching/speaking ministry. I didn't share this with anyone but my mother-in-law, who attended the conference with me.

Even during my battle with Cushing's syndrome, I knew there was more to life than "just" surviving. I felt that God may use my story in a way that would encourage others. At the time, it was hard to understand God's will in it all, and even when I felt His call, I didn't know what it would look like. Yet, I still trusted Him with the outcome . . . or did I?

Although I felt God's call on my life in 1996, it was a twelve-year wait until I received my first invitation to share at another church. Honestly, there were times I wondered *why. Why, God, have You not opened the door yet?* But during this twelve-year period of preparation, I would feverishly immerse myself in God's Word through multiple Bible studies, as well as work in various ministries. Each experience built on the previous one and prepared me for the open door God called me to enter through years later.

Sometimes I felt discouraged that God didn't move a little faster in the process. I wanted to hurry Him along. But through a tough lesson, God showed me that He wanted me to be willing to speak to one woman first rather than a multitude. What God wanted and what I thought were very different. Humbled by a song I was listening to while waiting to pick up my then preschooler, I heard God speak to my heart, "Are you willing to speak to one person?"

When I finally bent my knee to His plan and became willing to speak to just one person, God began His plan, not mine. What I thought would be a call to reach multitudes, God meant for an audience of one.

Likewise, at times you may wonder, *Is this what God wants from me?*

His calling on my life seemed to take longer to develop than I anticipated. Yet, through the waiting, I came to know God in a deeper way. He showed me more about Himself, and I realized that the preparation time was necessary for this season of my life. As I mentioned in a previous chapter, if I had stepped ahead of God,

> *Therefore, humble yourselves under the mighty hand of God, that He may exalt you at the proper time.*
> —1 Peter 5:6

it would have been a complete train wreck. I would definitely not have been prepared. Yet now, in His timing, I am walking in the fullness of His calling. I don't always know the next step, but I've learned to trust Him and just follow Him for the day ahead of me.

I share this personal story to say that God builds upon some of your darkest moments in order to accomplish His will. I know you may find it hard to embrace some of your experiences as God's plan. However, in every place a purpose exists, and it's up to you to experience this purpose to its fullest. Regardless of the situation, you can control only one thing—your attitude. Oh, others can affect your attitude, but you get to choose how you will respond. Will you have a Promised Land attitude, or a wilderness attitude? One of expectancy and joy, or one that displays complaining and *woe-is-me*?

If you can view your disappointments as Paul did in the first chapter of Philippians, it will help you walk out the days ahead of you. Verse 12 says, "Now I want you to know, brethren, that my circumstances have turned out for the greater progress of the gospel." Like Paul did regarding his imprisonment, can you look at what you have gone through and consider those experiences stepping stones to all God has for you? Paul continues in Philippians 1:21-24:

> *For to me, to live is Christ and to die is gain. But if I am to live on in the flesh, this will mean fruitful labor for me; and I do not know which to*

choose. But I am hard-pressed from both directions, having the desire to depart and be with Christ, for that is very much better; yet to remain on in the flesh is more necessary for your sake.

God has kept you alive and given you opportunity for fruitful living. Yes, fruitful living! So, what are you going to do with it? Are you going to live your life to your fullest potential? Or are you going to settle for ease and comfort? Revelation 3:7 (NIV) says, "These are the words of him who is holy and true . . . . What he opens no one can shut, and what he shuts no one can open."

Aim to please God and not man. If you choose to trust God alone, you will end up right in the middle of what God has called you to for this specific time and place. "Behold, He will do something new, now it will spring forth; will you not be aware of it? He will even make a way in the wilderness, and rivers in the desert" (Isaiah 43:19). What you do with the opportunities given to you is your gift back to God through your response, action, and commitment.

Take the leap? Ready or not, *let's go!*

Those prepared to do the work achieve a whole lot more than those who sit back and expect something to be handed to them. There is no reward for those who do not take a risk. As the old saying goes, "Nothing ventured, nothing gained."

I know that you may think to yourself, *But I have never gone this way before.* It's okay. Just don't let those thoughts paralyze you and stop you from experiencing all God has for you. Remember Søren Kierkegaard's quote from your personal development exercise in Chapter Two, The Walk: "Life can be understood backwards, but it must be lived forward."

Others will try to hold you back, but obey the voice of God and do not listen to the discouragement of man. Nothing others do or say should ever upset the one whose life is built upon God as the foundation. Remember this: God is for you (Psalm 56:9b). You must continue to move forward despite not being applauded and supported by those you think should be cheering you on. There will always be people you thought would be your biggest fans, but they turned out to be your biggest frustrations. One thing I have learned from experience is that you must be discerning about whom you share your dreams and desires with. Be cautious with those whom you are authentic and vulnerable because not every person is going to be as enthusiastic as you are about the dream God has placed in your heart. Oh, but once you find others with the same passion as you have, there is no telling what God can do with a few!

One of my favorite Bible characters is Joshua. Joshua was asked to do something he had never done before. After being mentored by Moses, he was handed the baton to take the Israelites into the Promised Land, along with Caleb. The mantle of leadership was passed from Moses to Joshua, so Joshua set out upon a new journey. Today, you may find yourself in this very situation of new beginnings.

Although the journey was new, Joshua had been trained by Moses, which prepared him for this moment—this challenge. Throughout Deuteronomy, we see Moses giving Joshua great instruction: power comes from the Lord (4:37); seek after Him and you will find Him (4:29); serve Him with all your heart (11:13); the Lord your God goes before you, to fight for you against your enemies (20:4); love the Lord your God, obey His voice, and hold fast to Him (30:20).

Furthermore, as you turn the pages from Deuteronomy to Joshua, God speaks directly to Joshua and explains what true success is. Joshua 1:8-9 says,

> *This book of the law shall not depart from your mouth, but you shall meditate on it day and night, so that you may be careful to do according to all that is written in it; for then you will make your way prosperous, and then you will have success. Have I not commanded you? Be strong and courageous! Do not tremble or be dismayed, for the Lord your God is with you wherever you go.*

The third chapter of Joshua records that he heeded all that he learned from Moses and heard from God as he set out on a way he had never passed through before. "Then Joshua said to the people, 'Consecrate yourselves, for tomorrow the Lord will do wonders among you'" (3:5). Joshua had a plan and executed it, and so should we.

- Make yourself ready for use (v. 5).
- Know Whose you are and Who goes before you (v. 11).
- Take the step needed (v. 13).

Sometimes God requires us to make the first move out of obedience to His call. I want you to stop for a moment and answer these questions.

- Are you ready to take a risk?
- Do you see the value of "today" versus the mentality of an eventual "one day"?
- Does change energize or paralyze you?
- Do you take responsibility for your life and decisions?
- Are you ready to finish what you started?
- Are you willing to do what others are not, even if that includes hard work?

Read Oswald Chambers' challenge at the beginning of his devotional, *My Utmost for His Highest*:

Have you ever "gone out" in this way? If so, there is no logical answer possible when anyone asks you what you are doing. One of the most difficult questions to answer in Christian work is, "What do you expect to do?" You don't know what you are going to do. The only thing you know is that God knows what He is doing. Continually examine your attitude toward God to see if you are willing to "go out" in every area of your life, trusting in God entirely. It is this attitude that keeps you in constant wonder, because you don't know what God is going to do next. Each morning as you wake, there is a new opportunity to "go out," building your confidence in God. " . . . do not worry about your life. . . nor about the body. . ." (Luke 2:22). In other words, don't worry about the things that concerned you before you did "go out."

Have you been asking God what He is going to do? He will never tell you. God does not tell you what He is going to do— He reveals to you who He is. Do you believe in a miracle-working God, and will you "go out" in complete surrender to Him until you are not surprised one iota by anything He does?

Believe God is always the God you know Him to be when you are nearest to Him. Then think how unnecessary and disrespectful worry is! Let the attitude of your life be a continual willingness to "go out" in dependence upon God, and your life will have a sacred and inexpressible charm about it that is very satisfying to Jesus. You must learn to "go out" through your convictions, creeds, or experiences until you come to the point in your faith where there is nothing between yourself and God.[1]

It is said of Oswald Chambers that he was a man who was *"never content with low achievements. . . always climbing the mountain peaks."* I once read a brief story of a man who died climbing the Alps' highest peaks. On his grave, after the climber's name, are these words: "He died climbing." Even though this is a short phrase, it had a huge impact on my life.

Do you have this same attitude? Whatever your hand finds to do, are you doing it with all your might (Ecclesiastes 9:10b)? Are you continually looking up and trying to strive for greatness? Or are there times when you adopt a "just-get-by" mentality? Leaders, you are called to a higher standard of living beyond yourselves. You are called to thrive, not just survive. All He asks from you is to come to Him with what you have, trust Him with the outcome, and He will do the multiplying.

In Matthew 25:1-13, we read the parable of the ten virgins, five of which were prudent and the other five foolish. The five prudent virgins were found ready, whereas the foolish virgins were not prepared, so they wanted to borrow the oil from the wise ladies. The foolish virgins had a "just-get-by" mentality. They were not found ready, and when they realized their lack in preparedness, it was too late.

Then in the parable to follow, in verses 14 through 30, you read about the talents. The master gave one servant five talents; the second, two; and the third, one. The first two servants doubled their talents, but the last man hid his one talent out of fear. The first two were blessed, but the last man's talent was taken away and divided between the other two men.

Both of these parables emphasize the importance of being watchful and prepared, as well as making good use of the gifts given to us by the Master. I desire to be among the five and two who are vigilant and wise. Don't you? Success is not just going to happen out of the blue, *poof!*—and all your desires and dreams come true without pursuit, purpose, and intent.

God wants you to do the following:

- Commit your ways to Him (Psalm 37:5).
- Practice the gift He has given you (1 Timothy 4:14).
- Be found faithful to the calling He has blessed you with (Ephesians 4:1).

When you commit your ways to Him and allow Him to determine the time and place of blessing, you will watch Him do "far more above and beyond what you could ever imagine or think according to the power working within you" (Ephesians 3:20). The power working within you from Ephesians 3:20 is the power of the Holy Spirit. Yes, you already have this power if you have received Jesus' love in your heart and confess Him as Lord! The Holy Spirit is a gift and has been entrusted to all who believe—not a reward to some. You just have to tap into His power and step out in faith. Embrace the Holy Spirit as your friend and guide. Luke 11:13 says to ask for more of the Holy Spirit and your heavenly Father will give Him to you. Stepping out in your calling will take a strength higher and stronger than yourself, so you will need the Spirit's power.

In the words of the TV show, *Extreme Makeover*, it's time to *move that truck*.

Take the next step.

It's time to leap.

Theodore Roosevelt said, *"Believe you can and you're halfway there."* Belief comes from a deep confidence that you have heard from God. Then, you must allow God to advance the second half. Maybe you are like me in that it has taken more years than you hoped before God opened the door of opportunity, or you have miraculously found yourself standing in the very calling He designed for you. Either way, it is time to act. In my case, I had prayed and prayed, so when the door opened, I knew it was the right time. Yes, I knew it without a shadow of doubt. Now, all I needed to do was walk through that door. Even though it seemed like more than I could handle, I had to follow God's lead and trust Him to continue to go with me.

It's not always easy, but you know that if you don't do it, you may burst. You have no other choice but to take the leap.

In the summer of 2010, I found myself in a new place. I had just resigned from a position I held for nearly nine years with an organization to fulfill the ministry God ordained so many years ago. This meant leaving behind co-laborers and familiarity, and facing many days of solitude as I transitioned to working in my quiet home. There I was with my new coworkers, Bella and Murphy, the furry golden-doodles, while I sat in my new office space staring at a blank chalkboard with plenty of thoughts running through my head.

So what did I do? I picked up a book. I typically don't read many fiction books, but this one came highly recommended, and it was exactly what I needed in order to take the leap. I encourage you to read *Dream Giver* by Bruce Wilkinson. This compelling modern-day parable will get you started on your own daring adventure, which is really a quest. The book shows how to identify and overcome the obstacles that keep millions of people from living the life they were created for.

Wilkinson introduces a character named Ordinary, who dares to leave the Land of Familiar to pursue his Big Dream. With the help of the Dream Giver, Ordinary begins the hardest and most rewarding journey of his life.

With this story, Wilkinson gives us practical biblical keys to fulfilling our own dreams, revealing that there's no limit to what God can accomplish when we choose to pursue the dreams He gives us to glorify Him. So, herein lies the question: Are you living your dream—or just living your life?[2]

Great things are what you will accomplish when you put God first and make Him owner of all you care about the most. And even if you feel like a Nobody, every Nobody is made to be a Somebody.[3] You can be one of the few who embrace that dream and pursue it with vigor, commitment, and the *I-will-finish-this-task* mentality.

Will there be days when you question your decision? Yes, of course. Those are the days you'll need to fix your eyes on Jesus and follow Him rather than your doubts. There may even be days when you listen to what others are saying rather than what God is telling you. But then you will need to choose to trust God even when fear reaches you through others' words or insults. Some of those people may try to intimidate you along the way, but like Nehemiah, you must not become discouraged and allow them to stop the work. Instead, allow God to strengthen your hands and march on (Nehemiah 6:9).

As you take the leap and trust God with the outcome, He will find you faithful. And little by little, He will call you up higher. He will set new dreams in your heart. For when you are faithful with a few things, He will put you in charge of many things and tell you to enter into the joy of your Master (Matthew 25:21).

> "I am the vine, you are the branches; he who abides in Me and I in him, he bears much fruit, for apart from Me you can do nothing."— John 15:5

However, what once was a dream can gradually become your own Land of Familiar again, so God may place a new dream in your heart. Will you be ready to take the next leap out of the familiar into the unknown? We can never become complacent because God is in the business of doing new things for and with those who stay connected to the Vine.

Friend, there is so much more ahead for you, too. I wonder how you will respond when that still, small voice comes to tell you it's time to leave Familiar again. I hope you reach for your new life with confidence. So many Dreamers do not. Once they've accomplished a dream, they settle in to enjoy it while trying to "own" it. No, it doesn't work that way. You are meant to keep reinventing yourself, your business, your ministry, your church, or your family. You were born for so much more. You are called to go after larger and larger dreams for God. And He will go with you. So when you hear Him say, "Come further," pick up your knapsack. Your horizon is full of promise. Another big dream is out there waiting for you, and if you don't pursue it, something important won't happen.[4]

I want to close this chapter with a front-row seat to a story from my husband John's life, as he sought after and embraced change while following his calling. Throughout my Bible, I see many handwritten notes next to *"wait"* Scriptures with dates and topics by them—some answered and others still waiting, some with tear-stained drops and others with smiley faces next to them.

One passage in particular stood out to me:

Delight yourself in the Lord;
and He will give you the desires of your heart.
Commit your way to the Lord, trust also in Him, and He will do it.
. . . Rest in the Lord; wait patiently for Him to act.
(Psalm 37:4-7)

Next to these verses I have written, "2013–John, softball coach." The note etched next to his name is, "God, you know." (When you dream big, you need to depend on God.)

My husband, John, worked in corporate America for thirty-one years. For twenty of those years, he coached softball for our daughter's Little League teams, their travel team, and yes, even their high school team. He then went on to assist with collegiate softball at a Division I school.

For the last six years of his business career, he planned his exodus from his sales position to begin a new career in full-time coaching. During this transition, he simultaneously completed his bachelor's degree online because he knew it would help him land a full-time coaching job at the college level.

In time, his big break came when the university where he had assisted for four years asked him to be the interim head coach for the final three weeks of the season. He graciously accepted and then began the application process to become the official head softball coach for the following season.

Wait. Wait. Wait.

As the interviewing process slowly moved on, the number of applicants dwindled from many to a handful to three. The nearly three-month period drew us closer to God and each other through dedicated prayer, trust, hope, and *waiting* since this opportunity was his greatest desire.

Our excitement grew when he was selected as the finalist and then named head coach. We then found ourselves walking down a road we had not traveled before. Filled with joy yet uncertainty, we celebrated and said good-bye to a past vocation.

Truly in John's case, success happened when preparation met opportunity. Yes, I understand this is a success story of someone who had a dream and sought that dream out, and then God opened a door of opportunity. However, it did not come without hard work, prayer, and determination.

But what about the other notations in your Bible that have yet to be answered? Are there dreams your heart holds onto but have not yet come to fruition?

You wait with great anticipation. "But," you say, "there is a *No* written next to the notation." I understand. I have a few of them too. They can be hard to swallow, but I keep coming back to the truth that *God knows best.*

I know that may seem like a lucid but difficult answer to a wishful dream. Yet, if you embrace God's will for your life, it will be easier to swallow.

I still believe when God closes one door, He opens another door better than what you expected. They may not have been your initial plans, but they were always God's plans. You just couldn't see them until He revealed them.

As with King David, the plan which was in his heart to build a house for the name of the Lord, the God of Israel, was just that—a plan in his heart. For it was his son, Solomon, who would be the one to actually build the house for His name and see it brought to completion (1 Kings 8:15-17).

> "For as the heavens are higher than the earth, so are My ways higher than your ways and My thoughts than your thoughts."
>
> —Isaiah 55:9

Sometimes another person may complete the vision God places in your heart. He just wants us to continue to be faithful with the days we have been given, and He will complete the work in His time.

As I finish this chapter, God has closed a door to a scheduled opportunity. And so now I must put into practice all I have written. It is never easy, but part of leadership is being able and willing to adjust.

As I awakened for my quiet time, my devotion found me in James 4. It was just what I needed to read and ponder on . . . . *Isn't that just like God?* No one can convince me He doesn't hear the cries or desires of the hearts of those who draw close to Him. My morning devotional verses were James 4:13-14:

Come now, you who say, "Today or tomorrow we will go to such and such a city, and spend a year there and engage in business and make a profit." Yet you do not know what your life will be like tomorrow. You are just a vapor that appears for a little while and then vanishes away. Instead, you ought to say, "If the Lord wills, we will live and also do this or that.

The door God closed may have been a *No* in my book, but in God's book, He already knew what would happen and maybe, just maybe, He wanted to see how much I had grown in my knowledge and trust of Him. My journal input for this day was: *I know You have a plan! Help me to walk in it*—Ephesians 2:10. *Give me wisdom to explore and seek Your direction.*

Life goes by fast, yet every day is willed by God, who is the one with the real plan.

Lord, help me to trust in Your plan even when there is a *No.* Indeed, as You say in Your Word, "For as the heavens are higher than the earth, so are My ways higher than your ways and My thoughts than your thoughts" (Isaiah 55:9).

A True Leap of Faith

Carl Eschenbach
Technology Executive, CA

After reading this chapter, I first spent time reflecting on the word "leap," a short yet powerful word that can be used in many different contexts. If used as a noun, it can be defined as "a sudden or abrupt transition," or if used as a verb, it can be defined as "springing through the air from one point or position to another."[5] Both definitions refer to movement and change. What I've discovered through my "leaps" in life is that to grow stronger you must leap further.

In recent years, God's call on my career has looked different. It was one which required a great leap of faith. But first, I want to share with you further about the leap I had to take in order to pursue that calling. This leap was one that challenged my faith in God and desire to pursue Him each step of the way.

When I initially realized my need for a relationship with God, I found myself asking many questions: How could one person (God) be able to accept anyone and everyone who wanted to leap to Him? How could someone be so powerful? How could Jesus be so accepting of so many simultaneously?

Making this ultimate leap of faith in the Lord is not something that just happens for people. This concept of taking a leap of faith means you're doing something with an uncertainty of what is to come. Personally, I think it's understandable that someone like myself would ask these challenging questions before making the leap. For those of us who finally do, we are reminded daily that this leap was the most important jump of our lives. As we continue pursuing this relationship, God requires many leaps, often daily, which provide opportunities for us to be instilled with greater trust in Him.

Over time, as my faith has grown, I realize these daily leaps of faith at times can drive us to our knees. In fact, I find the Lord doing that quite often. This is not His way of punishing us, but rather of strengthening our relationship and challenging us to leap even further. When I find myself in this place, I pray for a change in attitude and that He would bring about joy, perseverance, and maturity within me.

Just over two years ago, I found myself on my knees in the face of a challenge. My career had presented a difficult decision that would require me to not only take a leap in my faith but my profession as well. It was a decision I agonized over for more than three months. I literally prayed day and night for answers from the Lord, but I could never seem to get a consistent answer. The decision was similar to what Jessie spoke about when her husband John leaped out of the corporate world into the world of collegiate coaching.

For me it was a decision with three possible outcomes—stay with an existing company that I had been with for fourteen years, become a CEO with a new company, or do something completely different than what I had done in my prior twenty-nine-year career. Each potential outcome had its pros and cons, but after discussing the situation with my amazing wife and three children one evening, I realized which decision was obvious. When your family looks at you and says, "Honey/Dad, we want you home more, and we don't want you to miss the special moments of our lives," the picture quickly becomes crystal clear.

Although the picture was clear, I found myself still questioning what I knew I needed to do because it would require a leap greater than what I'd ever experienced. I then turned to my nightly prayer and asked the Lord to validate my decision and stand by me once I decided. The primary reason I asked Him to stand by me once I made the decision was that I have learned (and I knew) that He was the only one who would never let me down or leave my side. No matter what we think about people, friends, or any earthly creature, it's important to know that they will at some point disappoint us or let us down, but the Lord—no way!

I made the big leap to decline the position of CEO, leave my company, and enter a new professional career. In doing so, I now get to sleep in my own bed almost every night instead of spending more than half my nights in a hotel room somewhere around the world. My family is happy, I am happy, and I know the Lord is happy because I took the leap He nudged me towards; and we now walk this path together. Almost weekly my decision and faith are challenged as new professional opportunities come my way. Yet through continued talks with my family, along with prayer, I have obediently stayed on the path that I leaped onto two years ago.

So, what have I learned about leaping? I now know that if you leap or jump, you must always land. If you know you are landing in the arms of the Lord, you will never be destroyed, no matter how far you jump or how hard you land. Having the King of Comfort on the other side is a pretty cool feeling!

Self-Development

Day One

Take the Leap

In 1996 God called me to a speaking/teaching ministry. Remember that I mentioned it was a twelve-year wait? It was twelve years on my calendar, but God used each act of obedience as a stepping stone. The initial leap began at my home in a new neighborhood in 1998 with much uncertainty on my part. I had no idea what it would become or where God would take it. Many years have passed, and multitudes of women have been reached and sent out, not only through the neighborhood Bible study but the ministry as well. If God can use me, an ordinary stay-at-home mom, He can use you! So be diligent and passionate about what God has called you to do.

Is there something God is calling you to do? Do you feel Him tugging on your heartstrings to pass something on to that person you have been reluctant to talk with? Or do you desire to take the leap into full-time ministry, open a coffee shop, take a painting class, or make a job change?

Time is fleeting! Now is the time.

Read Jeremiah 1:6-9 and answer the following questions:

What was Jeremiah's excuse? Do you find yourself facing the same excuse?

What was the Lord's reply?

God reassured Jeremiah that he should not fear the people. Which people in your life do you fear? How has this Scripture encouraged you to trust God rather than fear man?

Now read Jeremiah 1:17-19. What added insight from this passage encourages you?

If you have a list of excuses as long as your arm and have not carried out what God is calling you to do, maybe that is all they are . . . excuses. Please take time to sit with the Lord and talk with Him to see if now is the time to carry out His plan. For such a time is this to make a difference in your family, home, community, church, and business.

Now I want you to write your answers again to the questions I asked you earlier in this chapter. Are you ready to take a risk? If so, how? If not, why?

Explain what the advantage is for "today" thinking versus the mentality of an eventual "one day."

Does change energize you or paralyze you?

Do you take responsibility for your life and decisions?

What action will you take to finish what you started?

Are you willing to do what others are not, even if that includes hard work?

Between your "once upon a time" and your "happily ever after" is NOW! Finally, take action. You have to start right where you are because tomorrow is not guaranteed. Right here, right now is the point from which you'll move forward.

Close out today by reading John 21:20-25. (If you are feeling ambitious, begin at verse 15.)

In your own words, what does John 21:22 say to you and how can you apply it?

Peter, curious about John's destiny, asks, "Lord, what about him?" Christ replies, "What is that to you? You must follow Me." In other words, "Don't look at others. Keep your eyes firmly fixed on Me!" These are the same words Jesus wants us to hear from Him: "Don't be distracted by others and their call. Follow Me!" God has a plan and a destiny just for you. Be still in His presence and you will hear Him. Continue to follow Him.

What is it that God is calling you to do?

Purposeful Action

If you have not established what God is asking you to do, wait. But if He has revealed it to you, take the leap. Create a plan, work hard, and stay the course.

Self-Development

Day Two

God's Timing

God may have given you a dream, but He doesn't always allow you to know the end result. He only requires you to be obedient with the step in front of you. At times, if you knew how long something might take, you might have given up. Although it's frustrating, not knowing the exact timing often heightens the suspense and builds anticipation. Yes, there are times you might feel like throwing in the towel because it is not happening fast enough, but you must learn to live in hope with great expectancy. Enjoy the season you are in as He continues to work out His perfect plan.

Read the following Scriptures and explain what they reveal about God's timing.

Psalm 37:23, 34

Proverbs 16:9

Proverbs 20:24

When God directs your paths, He sometimes leads you in ways that don't make sense, so you're not always going to understand everything. If you try to reason out everything, you will experience struggle, confusion, and frustration—but there is a better way.

Write and memorize Proverbs 3:5-6.

Is there something you and/or your team have been trusting in other than God's plan?

Are you trying to figure it all out on your own? If yes, what do you need to do to trust in God's timing?

Look up, memorize, and write the following passage on a sticky note. Do whatever it takes until this Scripture is embedded in your spirit.

Write out Psalm 31:14-15.

Your times are in His hands. Is that a hard one to swallow? So what do you do in the meantime? Lean in, rely on Him, and prepare as best as you know how so that when the door opens, you can walk through it. First Peter 5:6 says, "Therefore humble yourself under the mighty hand of God, that He may exalt you at the proper time."

"Proper time" refers to God's time. Remember, God may be delaying the outcome because He is still preparing you. Once you embrace the wait, the sooner God can work out His plan in your life, and then you can join Him in His work.

Read James 4:7-10 and list the cures for pride.

v. 7 _____

v. 8 _____

v. 9 _____

v. 10 _____

My pastor once taught on this Scripture passage and simplified it like this: "Give in! Get close! Clean up! Get down!" These are the four steps to humility. Continue to guard your heart against pursuing prosperity, prestige, and power rather than the presence of God. "For in His presence is where you will find the fullness of joy" (Psalm 16:11).

Is today God's plan for you to move forward? You and your team must establish the move.

Choose a goal.

Create a plan.

What work needs to be done?

Is there a deadline required?

Purposeful Action

I know there is a fine line between waiting and taking action. Figure out where you are and then be all in. If God shows you to wait—*Prepare*. If He tells you to take action—*Leap*.

Self-Development

Day Three

Prayer Works!

While sitting through a training session, we were given a passage from a not-so-common Bible version that hit me like a ton of bricks, and it became the foundation on which I built our team upon.

Read Psalm 16:5-8 (NET) and answer the following questions.

Lord, you give me stability and prosperity;
you make my future secure.
It is as if I have been given fertile fields
or received a beautiful tract of land.
I will praise the Lord who guides me;
yes, during the night I reflect and learn.
I constantly trust in the Lord;
because he is at my right hand,
I will not be upended.

Who gives you stability and prosperity, and makes your future secure?

What have you been given?

Who is your guide?

Whom do you trust?

What does your life represent when you allow Him to be your foundation?

What portion of this Scripture needs to be embedded into your mind and heart?

Yes, you have been given a beautiful tract of land where "the lines have fallen in pleasant places." Indeed, your heritage is beautiful to Him (Psalm 16:6).

Now that you have established that stability, security, and fertile fields come from the Lord, He may be asking you to move out into that beautiful land and take the leap. As you move out, ask Him to lead you each step of the way.

Read 1 Chronicles 4:9-10 and answer the following questions.

Whom did Jabez call upon?

Whom did Jabez acknowledge that blessings come from?

What did Jabez ask God to do?

Whose hand did Jabez find guidance from?

What request did Jabez ask to be free of?

Jabez said, *"Keep me from harm so that I will be free from pain."* The name "Jabez" literally means "born with pain." His own mother named him this because of the pain she endured in labor! When Jabez prayed, he spoke against the testimony of his name and let go of the shame it covered him in. Likewise, when you pray, come to God vulnerable and ready for Him to turn your weakness into His glory.[6]

Jabez was not using prayer as a formula to get something from God. Instead, he was calling upon God to help him accomplish the promises of God!

How have you implemented prayer into your desire and dreams?

How will your team make prayer a higher priority?

I know sometimes you might think you don't have as much time as you like for prayer. However, it is the most vital part of your meeting. When I look back on my younger leadership days, I realize how often I would tack prayer on to the end of a meeting. But as I developed my leadership skills, I realized that designated prayer was the most important bullet point on the agenda.

Instead of tacking it on to the end of the meeting, start your meeting with prayer. Hold prayer in a separate room from the strategic part of the meeting—away from the notes, agendas, and laptops. Incorporating prayer will create bonding within a team by taking the focus off of self and placing it on God and others, developing greater relationships between team members, and breaking down unnecessary walls. However, if you don't have the opportunity to engage in prayer as a team because you find yourself in a secular setting, be sure to pray prior to the meeting to help focus your thoughts and plans.

What will you do to incorporate prayer into your meetings?

If any, what changes will you need to make to embrace prayer as a team?

Purposeful Action
Claim the land God has provided for you. Ask Him to bless it and expand your reach. Incorporate prayer and watch God move.

Self-Development

Day Four

Arise. Fulfill. Go.

In Joshua 3 you will read how Joshua had a plan and executed it.

Let's make it personal. Read the following Scriptures from Joshua 3 and write what you and/or your team need to do to accomplish all God has for you.

v. 5

v. 11

v. 13

Sometimes God doesn't act unless you make the first move. Take the leap. Initiate the movement and God will provide the miracle.

Read the following Scriptures and record the meaningful
instruction received and result accomplished, if stated.

Colossians 4:17

2 Timothy 4:5

Hebrews 11:8

In the *New Living Translation*, 2 Chronicles 16:9a says, "The eyes of the
Lord search the whole earth in order to strengthen those whose hearts are fully
committed to him." Are you fully committed to Him, wholeheartedly devoted to
Him? Or do you find yourself half-heartedly seeking Him with all He wants you
to accomplish?

What will it take for you to give yourself fully to God?

**Do you need to lay something down at His feet? If yes, make a list
and share how you will approach it this week.**

Arise. fulfill. Go. The Great Commission wasn't just for the chosen eleven,
but it is also for you and me. And He has entrusted this very time on the kingdom
calendar for you to leave your legacy and imprint for those who come behind you.

Purposeful Action
**Become what God wants you to become, doing what God wants
you to do and having what God wants you to have. Move out with
His strength.**

Self-Development

Day Five

Take Action!

At the end of each chapter, Day Five will be a "take action day" for you and your team.

Write your personal goals.

Write your team goals.

Take the step in creating a plan.

When creating a plan, I typically start with the end goal in mind and work backwards to set a timeline for completion of the event, project, or occasion.

1. **What exactly are you creating? Be as specific as possible. (e.g. event, writing project, fundraiser, product launch, etc.)**

2. **When must it be completed by?**

3. **What resources (people, equipment, and budget) do you have access to for completion of the project?**

Chapter Four

THE TEAM

Two people are better off than one, for they can help each other succeed.
If one person falls, the other can reach out and help.
But someone who falls alone is in real trouble.
Likewise, two people lying close together can keep each other warm.
But how can one be warm alone?
A person standing alone can be attacked and defeated,
but two can stand back-to-back and conquer.
Three are even better, for a triple-braided cord is not easily broken.
(Ecclesiastes 4:9-12 NLT)

This book is designed for the busy leader in mind with four manageable chapters—short, but purposeful. However, you will find this last chapter has more content than the previous three, so hang in there. We have a lot of ground to cover as you build your team. Hopefully, with this last chapter you'll find yourself discovering your call, perfecting your walk, and finding the courage to take the next step.

You can't do it alone! It will take a team of people to advance your business, cause, ministry, or church to the next level. You probably don't need me to say this, but I will go ahead and say it anyway: *God has possibly given you a task that is beyond the ability of a single person.* As we have previously established, it is vital that the leader is passionate about the cause. If you are not passionate, you will not draw much commitment from others.

As you work through this chapter, you will see the importance of establishing a well-rounded team and enlisting like-minded people who are not exactly "mini-me's." You will learn how to identify and enlist those who have the same passion but different giftedness. Building a team with others who have different gifts and abilities will be the key to a diverse and successful one.

The famous Scottish-American industrialist, business magnate, and philanthropist, Andrew Carnegie, said, "It marks a big step in a man's development when he comes to realize that other men can be called in to help do a better job than he can do alone." Yes, there are some things that you as the leader will need to do, but there are plenty of other tasks, decisions, and needs that will only be accomplished through teamwork. You will want to involve others—their knowledge, wisdom, gifts, and callings.

You and I are not on this green earth to serve ourselves, but to serve God and others. As much as you would like to isolate yourself and try to go it alone, don't do it unless it is for a designated time away to search your heart, such as a personal sabbatical and development period. Otherwise, seek companionship and be a team player. Seeking isolation or taking on a *do-it-yourself* mentality will only bring exhaustion, resentment, and bitterness because the work becomes all about you. You will be most effective when you trust others to work with you in carrying out the mission. You certainly can become tired along with those who are called to be a part of your team, but if together you focus on the reward and not the difficulty of the work to get there, it will be more fulfilling.

Selwyn Hughes, best known for writing the daily devotional *Every Day with Jesus*, says,

When you have no understanding of what your basic gift is, then it is likely that you will go through life with minimum effectiveness and maximum weariness. When you do understand what your basic gift is, I promise you that you will go through life achieving maximum effectiveness with minimum weariness. Our leadership will always be most natural, most effective, and most influential when we lead from our gifts and strengths. Then it won't be forced, feel awkward, seem artificial, or copy someone else.[1]

Basically, he's saying, *Stay in your lane.* Know your giftedness and strengths so you can effectively work within them.

When seeking out potential team members, you will want to be observant regarding their gifts and abilities. In 2 Timothy 1:6-7, God uses Paul to encourage Timothy to keep rekindling the spiritual gift he has been given and not display a spirit of timidity, but of power and love, and a sound mind. The NIV says, *Fan into flame the gift of God,* and the Message Bible says, *Keep that ablaze!* As you consider this Scripture, be intentional to watch for those who are passionate about what they do and how they use the gifts they have been given.

Consider these three steps when inviting a team member to utilize their gifts:

1. First, find people who are working in their giftedness.

2. Once you have established their giftedness, observe them exercising their gift. Watch to see if they are fanning the flame and keeping it ablaze.

> *Since we have gifts that differ according to the grace given to us,*
> *each of us is to exercise them accordingly:*
> *if prophecy, according to the proportion of his faith;*
> *if service, in his serving; or he who teaches, in his teaching;*
> *or he who exhorts, in his exhortation;*
> *he who gives, with liberality; he who leads, with diligence;*
> *he who shows mercy, with cheerfulness.*
> (Romans 12:6-8)

3. Then, place them in a role where they will be energized.

When you build your team with those who know and understand their giftedness as they practice those gifts, you will be able to utilize them in the areas that allow them to thrive, which, in turn, will effectively move your team closer to accomplishing all God has planned.

Gloria McDonald, in her book, *High Call, High Privilege*, says, "Untended fires soon die and become just a pile of ashes." Not only do we need to tend to the inner fires, but we must also fan into flame the gifts He has given us. If not, they will become worthless and devoid of effectiveness.[2]

We also need to remember that whether it is a natural ability or a spiritual gift, everything we have is a gift of God's grace (Ephesians 4:7). Thus, none of us can boast in our gifts. (You will take a Spiritual Gift Survey in Day Two of your personal development exercise.)

As previously established, one of the most important qualities to look for in those you build your team with is a servant-leader attitude. You want your team members to be unified through humility. Philippians 2:1-4 states,

Therefore if there is any encouragement in Christ, if there is any consolation of love, if there is any fellowship of the Spirit, if any affection and compassion, make my joy complete by being of the same mind, maintaining the same love, united in spirit, intent on one purpose. Do nothing from selfishness or empty conceit, but with humility of mind regard one another as more important than yourselves; do not merely look out for your own personal interests, but also for the interests of others.

> You want those you work with to have a desire to make others feel good about themselves, rather than making them feel good about their own selves.

You want those you work with to have a desire to make others feel good about themselves, rather than making them feel good about their own selves.

One of my favorite books on leadership is *Jesus on Leadership,* by C. Gene Wilkes. In his book he says,

I realized that we who lead often overlook the fact that the true place of Christlike leadership is out in the crowd rather than up at the head table. People who follow Christ's model of leadership would never be embarrassed to find themselves among the kitchen help. Such a leader is comfortable working with those who serve in the background and gladly works alongside them until they complete the job. Head tables are optional for leaders who follow Jesus. Service, not status is the goal of this kind of leader.[3]

Another way of saying this is that the leader must be willing to take out the garbage as well as stand on the platform. Humble leaders will roll up their sleeves and do the mundane roles necessary to complete the job.

Eric Geiger, the senior vice-president at LifeWay Christian Resources, shares in an article the following three reasons humble leader are effective leaders, based on research done by Zenger Folkman, a leadership training company:[4]

1. **Humble leaders benefit from others.**
   Humble leaders benefit from the wisdom of others because they don't claim to have all the answers. They benefit from the giftings of others because they don't believe they have all the gifts. Humble leaders enjoy others, bless others, and are blessed by others.

2. **Humble leaders energize others.**
   Zenger and Folkman's research also discovered that leaders who underrate themselves have more engaged employees. Humble leaders will lead a more engaged team because they value the people, along with their perspectives and contributions. Humble leaders energize others because they know they need the gifts and contributions of everyone on the team.

3. **Humble leaders receive from the Lord.**
   St. Augustine is credited with saying, "God is always trying to give us good things, but our hands are too full to receive them." A humble

leader doesn't have full hands but open ones that are ready to receive wisdom, power, and mercy from the Lord. "The Lord resists the proud, but He gives grace to the humble" (James 4:6).

First Peter 5:5-6 also supports this style of leadership: "All of you clothe yourselves with humility toward one another, for God is opposed to the proud, but gives grace to the humble. Therefore humble yourselves under the mighty hand of God, that He may exalt you at the proper time."

When we desire to choose a humble-attitude approach, our leadership style will be more *other-centered*. Through the Scriptures, we are reminded of the high value Christ puts on relationships. John 13:34 tells us, "Love one another. As I have loved you, so you must love one another." When you are other-centered, your team will know that you care for them as people and they're not merely pawns on your board.

Okay, you might be thinking, from all you have read thus far, *this is all great, but unrealistic. Building a team like this is an A-level team, a dream team.* But isn't that the goal—fulfilling the goal of building the best team possible? "Build" is the key word. "To build" means "to establish and develop (a business, relationship, or situation) over a period of time." I certainly have learned the hard way about building a team. I have, at times, filled a position just to occupy it when I should have waited to fill it with the right person. It takes time to build your team, and it may involve removing people as well as adding them.

These are six important steps to consider when building your team:

1. **First and foremost, pray!**
   You may have all the people you think should be on your team, but they may not be who God has in place. You don't want to move ahead of Him. Don't force the issue if someone is hesitant. You will spend more time trying to convince and engage them when you should be focusing on other things.

2. **Consult a boss, pastor, or a person in higher authority.**
   There are times you won't know everything about a person. So, you will want to consult someone who may know that person better than you do

to see if they are fit for the role in their particular season of life. Doing this may prevent heartache in the end.

3. **Watch those you do work or ministry with.**

   Observe those you are considering to join your team. Pay attention to their attitude, character, and commitment level. Do they grasp the vision and mission of the company, ministry, or organization? Do they follow through with small tasks they have been assigned? Are they teachable and willing to receive counsel from others?

4. **What's their availability status?**

   Be careful when enlisting those whom you feel may be overcommitted. People are not meant to do a hundred things, but only a few that they do well. If they are really interested in joining your team, they may need to step down from something else.

5. **You want them to have passion.**

   Make sure they know the mission and vision of your organization and are able to articulate it well. It is a good idea to interview them so you can hear their heart and level of desire.

6. **Ask them.**

   If you have considered the previous five steps, you are now ready to simply ask. My theory is they can always say no. If you don't ask, you won't know. In one situation, I was hesitant to ask a woman to join our team because of her involvement in other areas. I knew she would be overcommitted if she joined our team, but as I prayed about it, I decided to ask anyway. Soon after we started our conversation, she shared how God was moving her away from a couple of other areas, so she felt freed up to join our team since it was where her heart really was. (I did follow up with her later to see if she relinquished her other positions before adding her to our team.)

An organization is only as great as its people. Believing many myths about leadership, people tend to fall into the trap of managing their team without influencing them. They become complacent about getting the job done rather than developing the company and people involved. To succeed, however, we must stand as leaders in our organizations, regardless of position, and influence the influencers.[5]

As you lead your team, it isn't so much about just getting the job done as it is building into those who follow you. You cannot effectively develop everyone, but you can influence those closest to you, and then those you lead will impact their followers.

We can learn from the greatest leader, Jesus, about whom and how to influence, from the people He walked with daily, to the multitudes. Jesus confided in *three*. He had an inner circle comprising Peter, James, and John. He took them on special outings and allowed them to witness His greatest glory (Matthew 17:1-2) and His deepest grief (Mark 14:33-34). He prayed with them (Luke 9:28) and taught them things He did not teach the others (Mark 5:37-43). They were His closest friends and confidants. They witnessed more of Jesus' private life than the others.

In the same way, this circle of companions will have the most dramatic influence in your life. They should be people whom you wholeheartedly trust and have the same mindset as you. This small team of people will be vital for your sanity. They will be honest with you and keep you grounded.[6]

Who are your three?

_____

Jesus trained the *twelve*. He chose the twelve disciples to be "with Him" and share in His daily life. He taught them and gave them assignments (Mark 3:14-15). Because of this, He entrusted them with power to do the work He Himself had done. In fact, He promised them that they would actually do greater works (John 14:12).

This team makes up an important part of your life and is critical to moving your organization forward. They are the people God has called you to shepherd, so they are under your leadership.

You pour into each other's lives. It can involve anything from a small team working on an event, to the larger group of four, seven, or twelve you empower to move your cause forward. When you lead and train your inner circle well, a ripple effect occurs as they begin to further your cause by influencing their own circles.

In 2015, More of Him Ministries celebrated five years of ministry. This was a milestone for our team. My circle of twelve from our *SHE Leads* leadership team surprised me with a celebration that will forever impact me. The setting was very intimate, with each woman sharing our time of ministry together. The night was a little overwhelming with grateful emotion and excitement for the future ahead. But this is what co-laborers do—encourage, uplift, and support one another.

Who are your twelve?

_____

Jesus mobilized the *seventy*, a close group to whom He gave specific service projects. He sent them out two by two (Luke 10:1).

This kind of team can represent your ministry, company, or service. These are people with whom God calls you to work on a specific task. Even though this is a larger group of people, it is a network that will support you and care for you. It is a group that can be broken down into smaller groups to accomplish more separately than together. But they always know their starting point.

Who are your seventy?

_____

Finally, He interacted with the *multitudes*. Yes, Jesus had a public ministry, occasionally speaking to thousands (Matthew 5:1). In today's world, these people are our Facebook friends, Twitter and Instagram followers, and Snapchat community. These are people we want to be a witness to, as well as an example of God's power through our changed lives. You would be wise to monitor what and how much you share with them. It is easy in today's social media-crazed world to overshare and regret it years later, if not minutes later.[7]

Who are your multitudes?

_____

Does this all seem a little overwhelming—the three, the twelve, the seventy, and the multitudes? You're not alone! In Numbers 11:14, Moses cries out to the Lord, "I alone am not able to carry all this people, because it is too burdensome for me."

Do you ever feel this way? Thankfully, there is a solution.

The Lord therefore said to Moses,
"Gather for Me seventy men from the elders of Israel,
whom you know to be the elders of the people and their officers
and bring them to the tent of meeting, and let them take their stand there with you.
Then I will come down and speak with you there,
and I will take of the Spirit who is upon you,
and will put Him upon them;
and they shall bear the burden of the people with you,
so that you will not bear it all alone.
(Numbers 11:16-17)

Likewise, Paul told Timothy to listen to all he taught him and then entrust those same teachings to faithful men who would be able to teach others (2 Timothy 2:1-2).

If you are feeling burdened, delegate to those you trust and allow them to take some of the load off your back. Your load will be lighter, but your team will be stronger as you invest in them, empower them, and entrust them with responsibilities. They will feel more appreciated and productivity will increase.

Delegation is a huge factor in moving your organization in the right direction. D. L. Moody said, "I'd rather get ten men to do the job than to do the job of ten men." I know there are things you feel you can do, and you may even be able to do the job better, quicker, and more efficiently than those you as

But if you don't delegate and then oversee that the job is done, you will end up frustrated, overwhelmed, and burned out.

Hans Finzel shares from his book, *The Top Ten Mistakes Leaders Make*, why leaders don't delegate.

- Fear of losing authority
- Fear of work being done poorly
- Fear of work being done better
- Unwillingness to take the necessary time needed
- Fear of depending on others
- Lack of leadership training and positive delegation experience
- Fear of losing value in the organization[8]

Not delegating basically comes down to fear. And what did we establish earlier in the chapter? We have not been given a spirit of timidity, but of power, love, and a sound mind.

Becoming secure in your identity and realizing you "are His workmanship, created in Christ Jesus for good works, which God prepared beforehand so that we would walk in them" (Ephesians 2:10) will help you trust that God knows the outcome. All you need to do is walk in it. It's already established, so join Him in His work.

When delegating, it's critical that you set others up for success. At times, failure will occur, leaving your followers feeling defeated. However, continue to guide them through the discouragement and point them toward the end goal. The best way for an individual or team to bounce back from a moment of failure is to walk out of the experience having learned something. This knowledge will empower them in situations to come.

In Exodus 18, Moses' father-in-law, Jethro, had come for a visit after hearing all the wonderful things Moses was doing. He rejoiced over all the good the Lord had done in Israel by delivering them from the hand of the Egyptians. But there was one problem he noticed immediately—lack of endurance.

Read Exodus 18:14-24. (I know this is a long portion of Scripture near the end of a chapter, but it is vital to your well-being, so please don't skim over it.)

Now when Moses' father-in-law saw all that he was doing for the people, he said, "What is this thing that you are doing for the people? Why do you alone sit as judge and all the people stand about you from morning until evening?" Moses said to his father-in-law, "Because the people come to me to inquire of God. When they have a dispute, it comes to me, and I judge between a man and his neighbor and make known the statutes of God and His laws." Moses' father-in-law said to him, "The thing that you are doing is not good. You will surely wear out, both yourself and these people who are with you, for the task is too heavy for you; you cannot do it alone. Now listen to me: I will give you counsel, and God be with you. You be the people's representative before God, and you bring the disputes to God, then teach them the statutes and the laws, and make known to them the way in which they are to walk and the work they are to do.

Furthermore, you shall select out of all the people able men who fear God, men of truth, those who hate dishonest gain; and you shall place these over them as leaders of thousands, of hundreds, of fifties and of tens. Let them judge the people at all times; and let it be that every major dispute they will bring to you, but every minor dispute they themselves will judge. So it will be easier for you, and they will bear the burden with you. If you do this thing and God so commands you, then you will be able to endure, and all these people also will go to their place in peace." So Moses listened to his father-in-law and did all that he had said.

Exodus 18:21 says, "You shall select out of all the people able men who fear God, men of truth, those who hate dishonest gain; and you shall place these over them as leaders of thousands, of hundreds, of fifties and of tens." You want to build your team with those who fear the Lord and are truthful and honest. Once you have established this network, then place them over thousands, hundreds, fifties, and tens. Then you will be able to face what is ahead of you with greater endurance.

Know your members' abilities and set them up for success by placing them over the amount of people they can handle and then giving them a role for which they have a skill set. Some may be able to manage thousands, while others only tens. You, as their leader, must be discerning as you watch them lead. Start new leaders with small teams, and as they grow in their individual roles, increase their responsibilities. Look to your seasoned leaders to bear more and help carry the weight of the organization. Each role is fundamental to the development of the individual, both personally and organizationally. Leading small teams or large ones can require a totally different skill set. Leading a small team is all about the relationships, ideas, and conviction about a cause. Leading a larger team can be more about strategy and vision, and can often become more of a financial leadership role as responsibilities increase.[9] So, knowing the skill set of your team members, as you can see, is imperative to the progress of God's call.

I want to close this chapter with an important but difficult topic for your team and organization. This may be as vital to the health of your team as enlisting members: knowing when to personally step down or when to ask another to step down. At times, you will inevitably find yourself in a difficult conversation with a team member when you're asking them to step down. It's not fun, and most people actually avoid it, which only makes things worse. However, as much as you may hate conflict, if the situation is not handled in a timely manner, good (healthy) members may step down due to the toxic environment.

It never gets easy, but over time you'll realize the importance of addressing these situations head on. A more timely and direct approach will increase trust, respect, and commitment from the other team members. Most of us can recount times when we fretted for dozens of hours, weeks, or even months, attempting to delay or avoid taking responsibility for a leadership conversation that must occur. However, sleepless nights can be replaced with one tough conversation. It's not easy, but it needs to happen. When you refuse to take responsibility in a tough moment, you will lose your ability to lead. If you do that often enough, over time, you will no longer be the leader. The person who will step up becomes the leader.[10]

The times I have had to confront others has always been for the betterment of the team and organization. I feel it is better to lose one person rather than five. Of course, you'll want to pray for yourself and the hearts of the persons you are approaching before meeting with them. Prior to the conversation, you will need to consider the potential outcomes. Certain individuals may agree and feel that stepping down is a mutual decision, while others may disagree with your assessment, which then forces you to remove them from their place on your team.

You will also need to realize going into the conversation that they may not receive your assessment, criticism, or critique well, and the end result will be that they do not remain on your team.

In order to create clear expectations of what it looks like to be on a team I lead, I prefer to provide job descriptions for each role that include details about the position and its primary tasks. By doing this, I've established a clear set of expectations that create accountability for each team member. And, if you happen to find yourself in a challenging situation that requires confrontation about an individual's status, you can refer to the mutually agreed-upon job description.

If you need to ask a leader to step down, you may find it helpful to work through the following steps to clarify your plan and guide that conversation in the best way possible.[11]

1. **Establish the Reason**

   It's important to discern the reasons why some people are no longer a good fit. Having concrete reasoning examples will provide clarity to the individuals with whom you speak. These are potential areas you may identify in those no longer fit for the role simply because you shouldn't take the same approach across the board when addressing the individual.

   • **Character** – They may have made, or are making, unwise decisions in their lives that warrants them stepping down.

   • **Competency** – They may not show the responsibility or capacity needed to carry out their respective roles.

   • **Chemistry** – They may not mesh well with the team, and even though this may not seem important, it definitely matters.

   • **Clarity** – There may be confusion about what their roles are exactly, so they're doing a good job at the wrong thing.

- **Gifting** – Gifting or wiring does matter. If certain individuals are serving in roles where they aren't using the gifts God has given to them, it may be a bad fit.

2. **The Approach**
Different reasons call for a different approach.

- If character is the issue, your approach should be to ask them to step away from their roles and focus on getting healthy. At the same time, however, you must serve them well by ensuring they are not abandoned simply because they aren't on the team. This is a time to lean in when others may walk away. Resolution and relationship is always the goal.

- If competency is the issue, you should provide training and accountability to determine if they can grow into their roles. The problem may be they haven't developed enough. Once you have provided training and accountability, you'll know if it's a fit or not. If it is not, you can redirect them to roles that fit them better.

- If chemistry is the issue, you should have a conversation with them to help them understand why their relationship among team members isn't what it should be. In some cases, this can be repaired if they adjust their attitude or whatever might be the main sticking point. Sometimes they are unaware of how they are perceived, so we just need to help them. However, chemistry issues oftentimes cannot be overcome, and the only solution is ask them to serve on a different team.

- If clarity is the issue, you have to start by evaluating how well you have communicated the vision and expectations surrounding their distinctive roles. Usually, there's more you could have done, and the next step involves coming to an agreement about what is expected.

In that process, however, you may find they are not a fit, so you'll have to ask them to move on.

- If gifting is the issue, you probably missed it earlier in the process. The good news is you probably have a better understanding of what their gifts are and can use that in helping them find new roles that are a better fit.

3. **The Process**

Every approach requires one key component—conversation. This is not fun, though important and necessary. It is poor leadership, as well as unloving, to allow people to continue serving in roles that are not a fit because it hurts them, those they serve, and the team they serve with. These conversations should be part of a process, not a one-off event.

If character is the issue, the process is unique. You ask them to step down in the first conversation, and every conversation after that exists to serve them and help them get healthy. In every other situation, there should be multiple conversations with a clear plan in place to help them before asking them to step down. A sample plan could include,

Week 1 – Conversation to specifically describe what the issues are and hear their input. The conversation should end with a clear plan laid out that's agreed upon by both parties.

Week 4 – Conversation to evaluate the last few weeks and determine if progress has been made. If it has gone well, point to the next conversation as another opportunity to check in. If not, point to the next conversation and the coming weeks as the last opportunity to see if this can work.

Week 8 – Conversation to evaluate the last four weeks and determine if they need to step down or not. If they have done well, more conversations can be set up to continue monitoring progress. If not, this is the time to thank them for their service and "free their future," as Andy Stanley says.

This process is purely a suggestion. You could condense the timeframe if you wish, but it's best not to draw it out longer than two months. The main point, however, is that the final decision to ask them to step down should never be a surprise. When you have the conversation, you may be tempted to soften the blow by generalizing things or referring to secondary reasons for the decision. Don't do that. Make sure you are honest, clear, and specific. Do everything possible to make it work, but don't be afraid to be bold and make the tough decision that's necessary for the health of your team.[12]

In the end, how you approach the conversation will set the tone for your remaining time together. Simply having proof or reasoning is not enough to have a positive conversation. It requires examination of one's tone, word choice, and nonverbal communication.

It has been my honor to share what I have learned and experienced through leading myself and others. I hope you have found these chapters helpful and purposeful, and trust that you are encouraged to continue leading well with a renewed commitment to abound in the work set before you and your team. May you have an I-will-finish-this-task mentality in all that God has set before you.

Therefore, my beloved brethren, be steadfast, immovable,
always abounding in the work of the Lord,
knowing that your toil is not in vain in the Lord.
(1 Corinthians 15:58)

The Team

Melissa Montalvo

Financial Consultant and Ministry Volunteer

Over the last ten years, I have been given numerous leadership roles in a large financial institution as a Certified Financial Planner™ and volunteer to local ministries. With all of my experiences I have learned how to both follow and lead. During the early years while following others' leadership, I was in training to pioneer and lead my own practice and, at times, my own team of volunteers. My life journey has helped me realize that I have always been in training—first, developing myself as a leader so I could understand the responsibility of leading well, and then implementing those same principles within my sphere of influence.

I can think of many essential qualities in gifted leaders, such as communicating a vision, leading by example, providing accountability, and offering encouragement. Yet, at the top of my list, I would say humility best reflects servant leadership. The apostle Paul wrote in Philippians 2:5-8 (NIV), "Your attitude should be the same as that of Christ Jesus: Who, being in very nature God, did not consider equality with God something to be grasped, but made himself nothing, taking the very nature of a servant, being made in human likeness. And being found in appearance as a man, he humbled himself and became obedient to death-even death on the cross."

There is a fresh aroma when humility is a character trait of a leader—in both corporate America and non-profit organizations. This is the hallmark trait of Jesus' life, and it should be for authentic Christian leaders as well.

The Team

Sarah Weimer
Manager, Large Health Network

As a millennial, I have had the opportunity to work in corporate America since I graduated from college. During this time, I have encountered fearless leadership, which inspires and motivates, while also stumbling upon quite the opposite. When I think about the best leaders I have followed, my current manager comes to mind. The qualities I see in him include humility, strategic planning, innovation, and empathy. I believe his mentorship approach, communication skills, and decision-making abilities have also played a vital role in his success as a leader. I think if you asked most millennials, they would say they're looking for a mentor more than a boss.

He holds me accountable, sets realistic goals, and works with me to develop creative solutions to obstacles I encounter, while investing in me within and outside of the workplace.

His coaching mentality creates an environment in which I'm willing to take calculated risks and learn from my shortcomings.

As we all know, work can be stressful, and sometimes we just need a break. Another manager developed a "pet board" in the office. If you overheard the conversations at the lunch table, you'd find that the team's pets are very near and dear to them. The manager identified this interest and decided to capitalize on it. Everyone from the team pinned a picture of their pets on this board. It not only allows you to bring a little comfort of home into the office, but provides a friendly face during a stressful day. This might seem trivial and silly, yet little exercises like this improve the overall camaraderie in an office.

Although I currently follow a great leader, I have also sat under poor

129

leadership. In hindsight, I believe this manager's shortcomings boiled down to a lack of emotional intelligence. He was unaware of how his actions and words affected those around him. Communication, as in most instances, was one of his biggest flaws. Although technology serves its purpose in business, it is important to have certain conversations in person, not through e-mail. His response to most situations were initially emotional rather than logical. Situations like this have taught me what not to be, while also allowing me to fully appreciate great leadership.

The Team

Pastor Brian Cooper

John Maxwell has rightly warned us that "everything rises and falls on leadership!" With that in mind, what I look for in potential leaders are these five traits. The first three are suggested by Bill Hybels, senior pastor of Willow Creek Community Church in Illinois. I have added the last two because I have found them to be helpful in my experience for recruiting potential leaders.

I look for character, chemistry, competence, commitment, and chronology. Are those I am considering committed to the organization, or do they chiefly use their roles as a temporary means to their own ends? Their commitment shows in their willingness to "go the extra mile" for the sake of the team by allowing their schedule to be interrupted in order to contribute to the team's goals.

Chronology has also been helpful. The longer we get to know potential leaders, the more we can see their character, chemistry with other team members, and competence to serve in their respective roles. At my previous church we hired six staff members, all from within our church family. We already knew them as they were able to get to know us. We worked alongside them in a variety of circumstances, and we knew them outside of church. All of those hires worked out very well. Some have gone on to other ministries, but we still look back on those times as special and a gift from God. It was amazing how smooth their transitions into leadership were.

I have also used another acrostic, often referenced around the internet, that indicates we should look for leaders who are FAT (Faithful, Available, and Teachable). In addition, I have added two more, making the acrostic FAITH.

The "I" stands for "Innovative." I want people around me who are looking for fresh ways to do what we are not currently doing and take what we are doing and make it better

131

through innovation. I like "idea people" because they bring vision to the team.

The "H" stands for Healed/ Humble. There is a consistency in their lives that comes with following the Lord instead of engaging in erratic, compulsive, or immature behavior. They are willing to learn from others, and know the importance of learning from the Lord.

Self-Development

Day One

Talents and Gifts

Building a team with members who are all-ins for the cause, ministry, or workplace is vital to the health of your organization. Now, I know there are times when people are only filling a position to bring a paycheck home or just occupy a role. It will be your job to observe your team members or employees and address the situation if it is less than par.

When building a team, it is good to know the members' individual giftedness, talents, and abilities. Everyone has some sort of innate talent. You may not think that you are particularly talented, but if you take a closer look at yourself, you'll discover there is some ability you possess in more abundance than others. Sure, there may be someone out there who is even better at this particular ability, but that's not the point. You *also* have an increased ability in this area relative to your other skills and aptitudes. Maybe you're a better athlete than musician, or maybe you're a better artist than mathematician. You know where you are talented and where you are not. But how do you know if this particular ability you're considering is a "natural talent" or "spiritual gift"?

Natural talents are those abilities inherited from one's parents and nurtured within the context of family. We all know talented people who come from a long line of family members sharing the same talent. Natural talents are just that— "natural"! They can be attributed to the natural genetic material existing within all of us, passed down from generation to generation. Spiritual gifts, on the other hand, come directly from the Spirit of God, which is the reason they are called "gifts" in the first place! First Corinthians 12:11 says, "The Spirit works all these things, distributing to each one individually just as He wills." Natural talents are imparted at our natural birth, whereas spiritual gifts are given when we are born again.[13]

Read the following Scriptures and identify the types of spiritual gifts they are.

Romans 12:6-11

1 Corinthians 12:7-10

Ephesians 4:11-12

1 Peter 4:11

According to 1 Corinthians 12:7, why are these gifts given to us?

How are you faithfully and fruitfully exercising the gifts you have been given?

Natural talents are honed by you and expected, whereas spiritual gifts are cultivated by God and surprising.

Let's say you are a talented leader, and you then become a Christian. If God decides to use you in some role of leadership, you just may find your talent is greatly multiplied when God also gives you the spiritual gift of leadership. You may now discover your leadership skills are above and beyond anything you were capable of doing prior to being saved. God has a tendency to surprise us in this way. We can all develop our natural talents with hard work and perseverance. As we practice and train along the way, we can achieve the expected results. Spiritual gifts, on the other hand, are increased as we mature in our relationship with God.[14]

What does Ephesians 4:14-16 reveal about your spiritual growth?

On Day Two, you will take a spiritual gift survey.

Purposeful Action

Make a list of your talents and spiritual gifts you think you've acquired. Are there talents that you have seen morph into God-given gifts? If yes, thank God for them and use them to your fullest ability through the power of the Holy Spirit.

Self-Development

Day Two

Spiritual Gift Survey

There are different kinds of gifts, but the same Spirit distributes them.
There are different kinds of service, but the same Lord.
There are different kinds of working,
but in all of them and in everyone it is the same God at work.
Now to each one the manifestation of the Spirit is given for the common good.
(1 Corinthians 12:4-7 NIV)

Now that you have established which spiritual gifts are available for Christians, it's time to see where you stand. Every believer—everyone who belongs to Jesus—is indwelled by the person of the Holy Spirit (Romans 8:9-11), who gives new life to sin-dead spirits. It is only through His presence that we are "born again" (Titus 3:4-7). As Paul clearly states, a spiritual gift is a specific way the Holy Spirit chooses to reveal His presence through the life of an individual believer.

Today you will answer a series of questions designed to help you discover your spiritual gift. A "spiritual gifts test" is a man-made tool meant to help believers discern their spiritual gifts. I personally like the gift test I took with LifeWay Resources. I have been granted permission to use this test for your benefit.

Additionally, I encourage you to take an online character strengths test. The VIA Survey of Character Strengths is a simple free self-assessment that takes less than fifteen minutes and provides a wealth of information to help you understand your core characteristics.

abound

Go to http://www.viacharacter.org/www/Character-Strengths-Survey to complete the survey.

Purposeful Action

God has anointed you to accomplish your task, but you are responsible for developing your gifts. Once you have discovered your spiritual gift(s), use them to your fullest ability and continue to practice them regularly.

SPIRITUAL GIFTS SURVEY

DIRECTIONS

This is not a test, so there are no wrong answers. The *Spiritual Gifts Survey* consists of 80 statements. Some items reflect concrete actions; other items are descriptive traits; and still others are statements of belief.

- Select the one response you feel best characterizes yourself and place that number in the blank provided. Record your answer in the blank beside each item.
- Do not spend too much time on any one item. Remember, it is not a test. Usually your immediate response is best.
- Please give an answer for each item. Do not skip any items.
- Do not ask others how they are answering or how they think you should answer.
- Work at your own pace.

Your response choices are:

5—Highly characteristic of me/definitely true for me
4—Most of the time this would describe me/be true for me
3—Frequently characteristic of me/true for me–about 50 percent of the time
2—Occasionally characteristic of me/true for me–about 25 percent of the time
1—Not at all characteristic of me/definitely untrue for me

_____ 1. I have the ability to organize ideas, resources, time, and people effectively.

_____ 2. I am willing to study and prepare for the task of teaching.

_____ 3. I am able to relate the truths of God to specific situations.

_____ 4. I have a God-given ability to help others grow in their faith.

_____ 5. I possess a special ability to communicate the truth of salvation.

_____ 6. I have the ability to make critical decisions when necessary.

_____ 7. I am sensitive to the hurts of people.

_____ 8. I experience joy in meeting needs through sharing possessions.

_____ 9. I enjoy studying.

_____ 10. I have delivered God's message of warning and judgment.

_____ 11. I am able to sense the true motivation of persons and movements.

_____ 12. I have a special ability to trust God in difficult situations.

_____ 13. I have a strong desire to contribute to the establishment of new churches.

_____ 14. I take action to meet physical and practical needs rather than merely talking about or planning to help.

_____ 15. I enjoy entertaining guests in my home.

_____ 16. I can adapt my guidance to fit the maturity of those working with me.

_____ 17. I can delegate and assign meaningful work.

_____ 18. I have an ability and desire to teach.

_____ 19. I am usually able to analyze a situation correctly.

_____ 20. I have a natural tendency to encourage others.

_____ 21. I am willing to take the initiative in helping other Christians grow in their faith.

_____ 22. I have an acute awareness of the emotions of other people, such as loneliness, pain, fear, and anger.

_____ 23. I am a cheerful giver.

_____ 24. I spend time digging into facts.

_____ 25. I feel that I have a message from God to deliver to others.

_____ 26. I can recognize when a person is genuine/honest.

_____ 27. I am a person of vision (a clear mental portrait of a preferable future given by God). I am able to communicate vision in such a way that others commit to making the vision a reality.

_____ 28. I am willing to yield to God's will rather than question and waver.

_____ 29. I would like to be more active in getting the gospel to people in other lands.

_____ 30. It makes me happy to do things for people in need.

_____ 31. I am successful in getting a group to do its work joyfully.

_____ 32. I am able to make strangers feel at ease.

_____ 33. I have the ability to plan learning approaches.

_____ 34. I can identify those who need encouragement.

_____ 35. I have trained Christians to be more obedient disciples of Christ.

_____ 36. I am willing to do whatever it takes to see others come to Christ.

_____ 37. I am attracted to people who are hurting.

_____ 38. I am a generous giver.

_____ 39. I am able to discover new truths.

_____ 40. I have spiritual insights from Scripture concerning issues and people that compel me to speak out.

_____ 41. I can sense when a person is acting in accord with God's will.

_____ 42. I can trust in God even when things look dark.

_____ 43. I can determine where God wants a group to go and help it get there.

_____ 44. I have a strong desire to take the gospel to places where it has never been heard.

_____ 45. I enjoy reaching out to new people in my church and community.

_____ 46. I am sensitive to the needs of people.

_____ 47. I have been able to make effective and efficient plans for accomplishing the goals of a group.

_____ 48. I often am consulted when fellow Christians are struggling to make difficult decisions.

_____ 49. I think about how I can comfort and encourage others in my congregation.

_____ 50. I am able to give spiritual direction to others.

_____ 51. I am able to present the gospel to lost persons in such a way that they accept the Lord and His salvation.

_____ 52. I possess an unusual capacity to understand the feelings of those in distress.

_____ 53. I have a strong sense of stewardship based on the recognition that God owns all things.

_____ 54. I have delivered to other persons messages that have come directly from God.

_____ 55. I can sense when a person is acting under God's leadership.

_____ 56. I try to be in God's will continually and be available for His use.

_____ 57. I feel that I should take the gospel to people who have different beliefs from me.

_____ 58. I have an acute awareness of the physical needs of others.

_____ 59. I am skilled in setting forth positive and precise steps of action.

_____ 60. I like to meet visitors at church and make them feel welcome.

_____ 61. I explain Scripture in such a way that others understand it.

_____ 62. I can usually see spiritual solutions to problems.

_____ 63. I welcome opportunities to help people who need comfort, consolation, encouragement, and counseling.

_____ 64. I feel at ease in sharing Christ with nonbelievers.

_____ 65. I can influence others to perform to their highest God-given potential.

_____ 66. I recognize the signs of stress and distress in others.

_____ 67. I desire to give generously and unpretentiously to worthwhile projects and ministries.

_____ 68. I can organize facts into meaningful relationships.

_____ 69. God gives me messages to deliver to His people.

_____ 70. I am able to sense whether people are being honest when they tell of their religious experiences.

_____ 71. I enjoy presenting the gospel to persons of other cultures and backgrounds.

_____ 72. I enjoy doing little things that help people.

_____ 73. I can give a clear, uncomplicated presentation.

_____ 74. I have been able to apply biblical truth to the specific needs of my church.

_____ 75. God has used me to encourage others to live Christlike lives.

_____ 76. I have sensed the need to help other people become more effective in their ministries.

_____ 77. I like to talk about Jesus to those who do not know Him.

_____ 78. I have the ability to make strangers feel comfortable in my home.

_____ 79. I have a wide range of study resources and know how to secure information.

_____ 80. I feel assured that a situation will change for the glory of God even when the situation seem impossible.

SCORING YOUR SURVEY

Follow these directions to figure your score for each spiritual gift.

1. Place in each box your numerical response (1-5) to the item number which is indicated below the box.
2. For each gift, add the numbers in the boxes and put the total in the TOTAL box.

LEADERSHIP	+		+		+		+		=	
	Item 6		Item 16		Item 27		Item 43		Item 65	TOTAL
ADMINISTRATION	+		+		+		+		=	
	Item 1		Item 17		Item 31		Item 47		Item 59	TOTAL
TEACHING	+		+		+		+		=	
	Item 2		Item 18		Item 33		Item 61		Item 73	TOTAL
KNOWLEDGE	+		+		+		+		=	
	Item 9		Item 24		Item 39		Item 68		Item 79	TOTAL
WISDOM	+		+		+		+		=	
	Item 3		Item 19		Item 48		Item 62		Item 74	TOTAL
PROPHECY	+		+		+		+		=	
	Item 10		Item 25		Item 40		Item 54		Item 69	TOTAL
DISCERNMENT	+		+		+		+		=	
	Item 11		Item 26		Item 41		Item 55		Item 70	TOTAL
EXHORTATION	+		+		+		+		=	
	Item 20		Item 34		Item 49		Item 63		Item 75	TOTAL
SHEPHERDING	+		+		+		+		=	
	Item 4		Item 21		Item 35		Item 50		Item 76	TOTAL
FAITH	+		+		+		+		=	
	Item 12		Item 28		Item 42		Item 56		Item 80	TOTAL
EVANGELISM	+		+		+		+		=	
	Item 5		Item 36		Item 51		Item 64		Item 77	TOTAL
APOSTLESHIP	+		+		+		+		=	
	Item 13		Item 29		Item 44		Item 57		Item 71	TOTAL
SERVICE/HELPS	+		+		+		+		=	
	Item 14		Item 30		Item 46		Item 58		Item 72	TOTAL
MERCY	+		+		+		+		=	
	Item 7		Item 22		Item 37		Item 52		Item 66	TOTAL
GIVING	+		+		+		+		=	
	Item 8		Item 23		Item 38		Item 53		Item 67	TOTAL
HOSPITALITY	+		+		+		+		=	
	Item 15		Item 32		Item 45		Item 60		Item 78	TOTAL

GRAPHING YOUR PROFILE

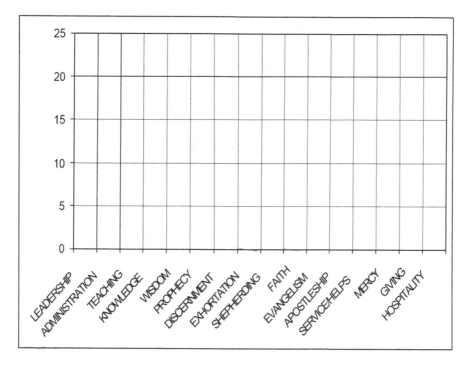

1. For each gift place a mark across the bar at the point that corresponds to your TOTAL for that gift.
2. For each gift shade the bar below the mark that you have drawn.
3. The resultant graph gives a picture of your gifts. Gifts for which the bars are tall are the ones in which you appear to be strongest. Gifts for which the bars are very short are the ones in which you appear not to be strong.

Now that you have completed the survey, thoughtfully answer the following questions.

The gifts I have begun to discover in my life are:
1. _____
2. _____
3. _____

- After prayer and worship, I am beginning to sense that God wants me to use my spiritual gifts to serve Christ's body by _____.
- I am not sure yet how God wants me to use my gifts to serve others. But I am committed to prayer and worship, seeking wisdom and opportunities to use the gifts I have received from God.

Ask God to help you know how He has gifted you for service and how you can begin to use this gift in ministry to others.

Self-Development

Day Three

Spur You On

Once you have completed your spiritual gift survey, list the top three gifts that are evident in your life.

Record your team members' gifts.

If you are working through this on your own, how are you working within your giftedness?

If you are working through this as a team, how are your team members working within their giftedness?

If team members are not working within their giftedness, prayerfully consider moving them into roles more fit for their work or ministry. Once team members are working within their unique giftedness, you will see an increased strength, enjoyment, and drive to abound in all they are doing so they will accomplish more individually and corporately.

After reading this quote from Selwyn Hughes, describe how it encouraged you.

"When you have no understanding of what your basic gift is, then it is likely that you will go through life with minimum effectiveness and maximum weariness. When you do understand what your basic gift is, I promise you that you will go through life-achieving maximum effectiveness with minimum weariness."

There are times you and your team members will grow weary. Yes, it may be because they are not working within their giftedness, but that is not the only reason. There are other factors that may cause weariness: motives may be wrong, expectations are set too high, self-recognition seeps in, or attitudes of pleasing man rather than God have taken over the process.

Read the following Scriptures and explain why your energy may be lacking.

Psalm 20:7

Psalm 147:10-11

Jeremiah 9:23-24

A good question to keep at the forefront of your mind as you make decisions is this: *Who gets the glory?* It can be ever so subtle. Do you boast in your gifts and talents and forget that every good and perfect gift is from above, coming down from the Father of lights, with whom there is no variation or shifting shadow (James 1:17)?

The great thing about God is that He gives us second chances when our first love is something other than Him.

Read Revelation 2:1-7 and answer the following questions.

What did Jesus praise the church at Ephesus for?

What did Jesus have against the Ephesian church?

What is the blueprint for returning to your first love, according to verse 5?

You and I can do a million things right, but if we don't do it with the right motive behind the work, it is not worthy of Him. Jesus gives us clear direction for returning to Him and our first love: Remember from where you have fallen from. Repent. Return.

Read the following Scriptures and describe how they spur you on.

1 Corinthians 15:58

2 Corinthians 4:1

Galatians 6:9-10

When we discover the root cause of our weariness, let us be encouraged to draw our strength from the Lord and not from our own effort. Let us also ensure that we do all things to glorify the Lord and remember that our reward comes from the Lord, not from ourselves or men. Then you and I will know our toil is not in vain in the Lord. And take heed from the great wisdom of Andy Stanley, senior pastor of North Point Community Church: "Devoting a little of yourself to everything means committing a great deal of yourself to nothing."

Purposeful Action
If weariness has crept into your life and work, discover the root cause of it and honestly examine your motives, specifically in the area where you are experiencing weariness in doing good. Are you earnestly seeking to glorify God?

Self-Development

Day Four

Encourage!

It's time to encourage your team. As a leader, you will serve those you lead by equipping them to do their part in God's plan while implementing these five steps, which will allow you to share your responsibility and authority as a leader.[15]

1. Encourage them to serve.
2. Qualify them to serve.
3. Understand their needs.
4. Instruct them.
5. Pray for them.

Equipping must be tailored to each potential leader. The ideal equipper is a person who can impart the vision of the work, evaluate the potential leaders, give them the tools they need, and then help them along the way at the beginning of their journey.[16]

Write each team member's name and a tangible way you can encourage him/her.

Member(s) Name   **Encouragement**

Member Name(s)	Encouragement

Please remember it is not all about you. It's about accomplishing all God has for you, your organization, or ministry as a team.

Read 1 Corinthians 3:1-9 and answer the following questions.

What is the result of walking in the flesh (vv. 1-3)?

Who gives you opportunities (v. 5)?

Who causes the growth (vv. 6-7)?

The labors of Paul or Apollos would have been fruitless if God had not been at work all along. You and I would do well to recognize that we can engage in ministry only by trusting that God will be at work, in and through what we do, to bring about the growth that God wants. If the work we are engaged in is built on some other conviction, we should remember, repent, and return.

Jealousy has no place in your life as a leader. You will want to build into those that follow you, encouraging them to reach for their dreams and walk out with great confidence all that God has called them to fulfill.

Read Deuteronomy 6:10-12 and write what you need to be watchful of.

As you and your team continue to labor for the Lord, remember where you have come from, all that you have been forgiven of, and who supplies the growth. Yes, "it is the Lord your God who brought you out of Egypt with His mighty hand and by an outstretched arm" (Deuteronomy 5:15). Success come from God. You would be wise to remember this.

Finish out this study by writing Colossians 1:25.

What was Paul's ministry and what was his attitude?

This verse gives us the answer to what constitutes a God-given ministry: having a servant's heart and recognition that God has *invited* us to be responsible for our lives and resources. We are not likely to manage well unless we acknowledge that we are managers. We are not likely to exercise good stewardship unless we recognize that we are stewards. There are many definitions of servanthood, but recently I read one that put the icing on the cake for me: "becoming excited about making other people successful."[17] When we serve others with hearts filled by Christ, we won't care who receives the praise, compliments, or recognition. In addition, we will be good stewards of the gifts and jobs that have been entrusted to us.

Purposeful Action

Be watchful of areas where you can encourage another family member, co-worker, ministry partner, or friend.

Self-Development

Day Five
Take Action!

Today marks the last chapter and "take action day" for you and your team.

I would like you to write the areas that you have worked on throughout this book and where you have seen growth.

Individual growth

Corporate growth

He has shown you, O man, what is good.
And what the Lord require of you?
To act justly and to love mercy and to walk humbly with your God.
(Micah 6:8)

Thank you for the honor of journeying through this book together with you. I know God will bless your diligence and commitment. As you increase in wisdom, He will move you and your team to the next level.

May the Lord give you increase,
You and your children.
May you be blessed of the Lord,
Maker of heaven and earth.
(Psalm 115:14-15)

Notes

Chapter One: The Call

1. Douglas K. Smith, "The Following Part of Leading," in *The Leader of the Future*, ed. Frances Hesselbein, Marshall Goldsmith, and Richard Beckhard (San Francisco: Jossey-Bass, 1997), 199-200.
2. Max DePree, *Leadership Jazz* (New York: Doubleday, 1992), 51.
3. Leith Anderson, *A Church of the Twenty-First Century* (Minneapolis: Bethany, 1992), 222.
4. C. Gene Wilkes, *Jesus on Leadership: Timeless Wisdom on Servant Leadership* (Nashville: LifeWay Press, 1998), 75-76.
5. Ibid., 18.
6. Pastor Jerry Edmon, sermon preached at Family Worship Center, Elgin, Texas.
7. Hans Finzel, *Top Ten Ways To Be a Great Leader* (Colorado Springs: David C. Cook, 2017), 44-47.
8. Ibid., 44-47.
9. C. Gene Wilkes, Jesus on Leadership: Timeless Wisdom on Servant Leadership (Nashville:LifeWay Press, 1998), 19-20.

Chapter Two: The Walk

1. James Strong, *The New Strong's Exhaustive Concordance of the Bible*; John Walvoord and Roy Zuck, *The Bible Knowledge Commentary: New Testament* (Colorado Springs: Cook Communications Ministries, 1983, 2000), 671.

2. Oswald Chambers, *Daily Readings from My Utmost for His Highest* (Nashville: Thomas Nelson, 1993).

3. "John Maxwell on Leadership," The John Maxwell Company, July 8, 2013, www.johnmaxwell.com/blog/7-factors-that-influence-influence.

4. Catherine Chen, Ph.D, "The Difference between Perfection and a Healthy Pursuit of Excellence," www.TheHuffingtonPost.com , 24 Aug. 2013, Web 30 Jan. 2017.

5. Marc Winn, "Perfectionism vs. Excellence," *The View Inside Me*, n.p., 27 Feb. 2013, Web. 30 Jan. 2017.

6. J. C. Maxwell and Tim Elmore, "Judges 6:11-8:35," *Maxwell Leadership Bible* (Nashville: Thomas Nelson, 2014).

7. Ibid.

8. Stephen R. Covey, *Principle-Centered Leadership* (New York: Simon and Schuster, 1992), 181-189.

9. Max DePree, *Leading without Power* (San Francisco: Jossey-Bass, 1997), 134.

10. Warren Bennis, *On Becoming a Leader* (San Francisco: Jossey-Bass, 1989), 41, 164-67.

11. C. Gene Wilkes, *Jesus on Leadership: Timeless Wisdom on Servant Leadership* (Nashville: LifeWay Press, 1998), 70-71.

12. Dr. Hans Finzel, *The Power of Passion in Leadership* (Highlands Ranch, CO: Top Ten Enterprises Publishing, 2015), 207.

13. Ibid., 213.

14. "Propel Women—Propel Women." *Propel Women—Propel Women*, www.propelwomen.org/.

15. Paul Kemp, *Quora*, n.p., 18 Apr. 2016, Web. <https://www.quora.com/What-is-the-difference-between-listening-to-and-hearing-the-word-of-God>.

16. Selwyn Hughes, "Every Day With Jesus," *Pursuing God*, January/February 2018, UK: CWR, 2018.

Chapter Three: The Leap

1. Oswald Chambers, *Daily Readings from My Utmost for His Highest* (Nashville: Thomas Nelson, 1993).

2. Bruce Wilkinson, *Dream Giver* (Colorado Springs: Multnomah Books, 2003).

3. Ibid., 69, 136.

4. Ibid., 156.

5. http://www.thesaurus.com

6. "The Prayer of Jabez – 5 Inspiring Lessons," Crosswalk.com, Salem Web Network, 14 June 2016, www.crosswalk.com/faith/prayer/prayers/the-prayer-of-jabez-5-inspiring-lessons.html.

Chapter Four: The Team

1. John C. Maxwell, *The Maxwell Leadership Bible: New King James Version* (Nashville: Thomas Nelson, 2007), 1508.

2. Gloria McDonald, *High Call, High Privilege* (Peabody, MA: Hendrickson Publishers, Inc. 1998), 13.

3. C. Gene Wilkes, *Jesus on Leadership: Timeless Wisdom on Servant Leadership* (Nashville: LifeWay Press, 1998), 13-14.

4. Eric Geiger, "3 Reasons a Humble Leader Is an Effective Leader," Eric Geiger, 22 Jan. 2018, ericgeiger.com/2018/01/3-reasons-a-humble-leader-is-an-effective-leader/?inf_key=fae6df66c415d11aaa2a7e7a-20docd8061ccc894ff8d4f16f99644301ced05

5. The John Maxwell Company, July 8, 2013, "John Maxwell on Leadership," *The John Maxwell Company*, 8 July 2018, www.johnmaxwell.com/blog/7-factors-that-influence-influence.

6. Michael Hyatt, "The Leadership Strategy of Jesus," *Michael Hyatt*, n. p., 24 Mar. 2010, Web. 30 Jan. 2016.

7. Ibid.

8. Hans Finzel, *The Top Ten Mistakes Leaders Make* (Colorado Springs: David C. Cook, 2007), 113.

9. John Brandon, "5 Signs You Need to Step Down From a Leadership Role," *Inc.com*, Inc., 7 Aug. 2015, www.inc.com/john-brandon/5-signs-you-should-step-down-from-a-leadership-role.html.

10. Dan Reiland, "How To Face Tough Conversations," Dan Reiland, 12 Feb. 2018, danreiland.com/how.to.face.tough.conversations/.

11. Nick Blevins, "Difficult Conversations: Asking Leaders to Step Down," *Orange Leaders*, 30 May 2017, orangeblogs.org/orangeleaders/2017/05/30/difficult-conversations-asking-leaders-step/.

12. Ibid.

13. J. Warner Wallace, "The Difference Between 'Natural Talents' and 'Spiritual Gifts,'" *Cold Case Christianity*, 26 Oct. 2017, coldcasechristianity.com/2014/the-difference-between-natural-talents-and-spiritual-gifts/.

14. Ibid.

15. C. Gene Wilkes, Jesus on Leadership: Timeless Wisdom on Servant Leadership (Nashville: LifeWay Press, 1998), 189.

16. John Maxwell, *Developing the Leader around You* (Nashville: LifeWay Press, 1995). 84.

17. Selwyn Hughes, "Every Day with Jesus," *Complete in Christ*, March/April 2008 (UK: CWR, 2008).

Meet the Author

Jessie Seneca is a national speaker, author, leadership trainer, and the founder of More of Him Ministries and SHE Leads Conference. She has been leading in the community and churches for over twenty-five years, as well as serving as a frequent YOU Lead presenter with LifeWay. Jessie and her husband, John, live in Bethlehem, Pennsylvania. They have two adult daughters and wonderful sons-in-law. Most days you will find her walking her two golden-doodles, Bella and Murphy.

The Secret Is Out

Learn it. Live it. Pass it on.

Did you know that God has a secret? One day, while Jessie Seneca was reading Colossians 1:27 in the New Living Translation (NLT), she saw it. There it was, God's secret: "Christ lives in you. This gives you assurance of sharing in His glory." Once you know it, you will never be the same. You can enter into a wholehearted relationship with the supreme and all-sufficient Christ. This study features five weeks of personal, daily assignments and six weekly group sessions with DVD (available separately). As this study guides you into a deeper relationship with your heavenly Father and Savior, Jesus Christ, you will be grounded in the truth of Christ, the person of Christ, and the power of Christ. You will be challenged in your everyday relationships—in the home, workplace, and church. Read and study the short yet compelling and powerful letter to the Colossians. When you are finished studying it, you will not only want to learn the secret for yourself, but live it out and pass it on. A companion DVD and audio CD are available for this title.

Road Trip

A personal journey through life's
detours and pit stops

Are you "living life" and wondering where all your plans went, only to realize that God's plans were always your plans and you just didn't see it? *Road Trip* is Jessie's journey in her battle with Cushing's syndrome, a life-threatening disease. Her story looks back at her ride through the ups and downs of her struggles, how God brought her through them victoriously, and how He is using her experiences for His purposes.

This book encourages you to see God's big picture in your own life and appreciate the detours and pit stops along the way that will help make you stronger and live a more purpose-filled life. *Road Trip* includes a study guide for personal reflection or group discussion.

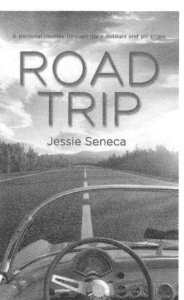

Joseph

A Life of Rejection, Resilience and Respect

Are you in need of a "pick me up" adjustment? Maybe you have been touched by rejection, shattered dreams, or are presently going through hard times. Studying the life of Joseph will help you understand the relevance of Joseph's experiences—from rejection and hurt to God's sovereignty, every step of the way. As you read and study about this most popular and beloved Bible character, you will find your own place in the journey and see God's plan fulfilled in and through your life. You will come out on the other side with hope, encouragement, and compassion.

This study features six weeks of personal daily assignments and seven weekly group sessions with the DVD teaching (available separately).

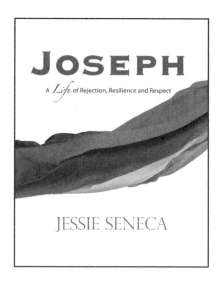

Friendship

Sisters for a Journey

The ride through life is better with friends! *Friendship: Sisters for a Journey* will help you discover the secret to authentic friendship through meaningful and purposeful relationships. Sometimes it might look a little messy and other times glorious, but God uses all styles and seasons of friendships to grow and stretch us into better friends, sisters, mothers, daughters, aunts, grandmothers, and any other roles we fill. With discussion questions at the end of each chapter, biblical application, and real-life examples, this book will help you be the friend you desire to be.

Raising Girls
Diaper to Diamond

Mom. Three simple letters, when put together, give you a life-changing title. Raising a daughter is one of the greatest blessings God can give, and He chose you for the unique role to teach His ways and pass down biblical womanhood to future generations. No one can do it quite like you, Mom! While writing *Raising Girls: Diaper to Diamond,* Jessie Seneca had one question at the forefront of her mind, "What do I wish I could tell the younger me?" Jessie, who has raised two daughters, draws truth and guidance from Scripture, personal experience and practical insights from other moms. She doesn't claim to have all the answers. Like most of us, she has made mistakes along the way, but her continued desire is to see girls develop into responsible, faith-filled women.

With discussion questions at the conclusion of each chapter, you'll feel empowered with thought-provoking conversations addressing a wide variety of topics such as dating, mean girls, self-image, perfectionism, a father's role and much more. Oh, and don't forget about that de-parenting stage we all experience as our daughters leave the safety of our homes to conquer the world in front of them. May you rise up and embrace this special calling of motherhood!

RAISING GIRLS

Diaper to Diamond

Jessie Seneca
Foreword by Arlene Pellicane
author of *31 Days to Becoming a Happy Mom*

Order Info

For autographed books, bulk order discounts,
or to schedule speaking engagements, contact:

Jessie Seneca
jessie@jessieseneca.com
610.216.2730

To order any of Jessie's books, visit
www.MoreofHimMinistries.org

Also available from your favorite bookstore and
Amazon.
Like us on social media:

Fruitbearer Publishing, LLC
302.856.6649 • FAX 302.856.7742
info@fruitbearer.com
www.fruitbearer.com
P.O. Box 777, Georgetown, DE 19947

Made in the USA
Middletown, DE
21 August 2019